Jiu Jitsu Chick
L. Dawn

Jiu Jitsu Chick
Copyright © 2020 by L. Dawn
All rights reserved. No part of this book may be reproduced or transmitted in any form or by any means without written permission from the author.

Photography- Kat Bradshaw
Graphics Design- Danyce Rodriguez

Printed in USA

0

All it takes is an idea. Changing the world, is that easy. Could I? Should I? Will I? At 8 years old, I had an idea: I wanted to make people smile, with my words. A smile, I believe, is the other half of a rainbow.

At age 10, my words began to ink themselves into blue lined pages.

At sweet 16, the words, "I want to change the world," answered the question of how to bridge the gap between the desires of my heart, and the dreams of my mind. As soon as the words left the getaway of my lips, I believed with all my heart and mind, I could, somehow. Even though I didn't know how. Now, at 31 years old, I have 3 big binders full of essays, poems, and songs. Ideas, dreams, and stories, a few nightmares in between.

Now, at 31, I have lived a fairytale I never dreamed I would live. Now, I have written my life into this storybook.

I have a dream. A dream I can change the world. A dream I can show the world, what love really is. What I feel it to be. What I learned it to be. What I now know it is.

With Love, all things are possible. I've seen it. I believe, with Love, the best happy ending, for all of eternity, can be.

CHAPTERS OF LIFE

1	1 Time Capsule	1
2	Who Am I 2 You	3
3	3 Martial Arts Story	5
4	4 Allen Clark	9
5	5 Secret Shame	14
6	6 Sides to My Love Life	19
7	7 Decembers Dancing	28
8	January's F8th	50
9	February's Life L9	70
10	March 10 Steps	99
11	April is 11 Heaven	118
12	12 May be a Lucky Number	135
13	13 Reasons June Can	149
14	Thank You Letters	179
15	Time Capsules	182
16	My Clean Little Victories	184
17	Dancing with Lightning	187
18	Love's Never Ending	189
19	Satan's Happy Ending	192
21	My Happy Be	193
22	About the Author	194

1 TIME CAPSULE

Dear Lady,

You did it. You made the first step. You are now a little bit further in the right direction.

I'm going to tell you a fairytale. My fairytale, though not the one I ever dreamed I would live, much less love.

I wish I could tell you love doesn't hurt, but it does. The pain comes from it bleeding through all the little broken pieces. That's what love does: it fills in the gaps. What we see as cracks, or the zigzag line down the middle of a broken heart, are the footsteps of love, making us whole again. Love becomes the golden thread holding us together. Love becomes the fire inside giving us drive and light. Love, becomes us.

For 30 years I loved everyone else more than myself for reasons you'll read within this storybook. For 30 years I stood at the ends of fingertips exclaiming blame, saying I was little more than "guilty." For most of my life, I believed them.

They say love is blind. I believe that's true. I believe love is blind because it sees the person, not the personality. The red flags, we as women don't see, or choose to ignore, because we are too busy looking for the signs. The signs pointing the way to our Prince Charming, our Fairytale, and our Happily Ever After.

Some love stories don't end with a Prince. Mine didn't. Mine ended the same way it began: with me. At the beginning I was battered, broken, and my heart was bleeding. In the end I was happy, healed, and my heart was beating strong. I'm still living some of my happy endings. As life goes on, they never seem to end.

My happy endings didn't just happen. I had to fight for them. Martial arts was my first love, my other half, the best part of me. After my Prince who turned into a Beast, left me, I returned home to my dojo, to Allen Clark, my hero, the only place I knew I wanted to go. It was there I fought my memories, my PTSD, my nightmares, my insecurities. It was the only thing I knew I wanted to do. I didn't want to sit in therapy, just talking it through. I wanted to do something. So, I did.

I can't give you all the answers on how to fight for or live your own happy ending. I can't even give you ten or twelve steps to take because, as you'll read, steps were taken every day. All I can do is leave a barefooted path, on the road I traveled. All I can do is tell you it led to a happy end. The choice to follow is up to you.

I can tell you it is worth it. Worth every bruise, bump, and boo-hoo. Worth every minute and milestone, you push and pull through. It's true, what they say, everything you've ever wanted, is on the other side of fear. I know it, because I lived it.

Life is blunt, and sharp, myself, and my words will be too. There are no disclaimers or warnings that can prepare you for the pictures your mind will paint with my words. Pictures your mind might not want to see. Fair warning: it gets pretty ugly.

Over the line fear draws in your face, through the life you never thought you could face, a whole new wonderful world, awaits. I double dog dare you, to turn the next page.

One word, three letters, say it, and life changes. Say "Yes." Please?

Love,

L

Dear Little Leslie,

Love yourself more, drink and think a little less.

Believe in yourself. Your gut knows the difference between butterflies and moths.

Don't listen to voices telling you that you can't. You aren't driving your life to a dead end.

Trust God, He knows what He is doing. Girl if you even had a clue you probably wouldn't believe the Fairytale He has written for you. You are so much stronger than the Damsel in Distress role you love to play.

Prince Charming is overrated. Your long hair looks prettier flying in the wind on the back of a white horse, than his ever did.

It will be hard but it will be worth it. Just keeping loving with your little big heart.

Love you,

L

WHO AM I 2 YOU?

I'm the girl who knew better, and the woman who chose wrong. As life lived and I grew, I learned, loved, and grew up.

Who am I? Well as life and time count onward and upward, so did I. Here, for the sake of understanding, is my lifeline.

1	Year-old, the first and only girl of three brothers to come
2	Big bouncy curls, I looked like a doll
3	Dolls became babies, as my world took shape
4	I danced
5	Princesses in the movies, added tiaras and twirls to my life
6	Stories from my books, shaped playtime
7	Prince Charming had no name, but in my mind, he had a face.
8	I found my dream
9	Princesses became real, when I learned a real life one had died
10	I wrote my first song
11	A white picket fence began building in my mind
12	Believing true love, once found, would never leave me alone
13	Believing true love, solved everything
14	Wanting to be the Princess, not the hero
15	Buried in homeschool and library books
16	Falling in love for the first time, with martial arts
17	Training and feeling a burn that didn't hurt
18	Leaving home, and losing myself in the world
19	Reunited with my family, life was calm
20	Cussing God out, because He had been hurting my feelings for so long
21	Bar doors opened up, I don't remember much

22	Disappointed I hadn't found my Prince Charming yet, according to my life plan
23	Raped while I was sleeping
24	Resigned to life alone, college bound so I could one day buy a pink home
25	A Princess, finally having found my Prince
26	My Prince had turned into a Beast
27	A Damsel in Distress
28	Praying for a miracle
29	My Fairytale ended
30	Going back to my first true love: martial arts, under the wing of my hero, Allen Clark
30	Fighting back against my memories
30	Turning make-believe, into manifest destiny
30	Hurting, burning, and thriving, going skydiving
30	The best year of my life
30	Damsel in Distress, turned back into a pretty Princess

The stories in this book are all based on true events. Certain details have been changed to protect the identity, privacy, and pride of those involved. I am merely writing my view, from my memory. The memories I question the truth of, I did not write. Some memories I believe the brain erases for us, those too bad to be fact.

This book is not meant to be a burn book; we are all the "bad guy" in someone's story. But rather this book is meant to leave a barefooted print, hopefully, for others to follow in. By following in the footsteps of my hero, and my God, I found a way to a happy ending.

3 MARTIAL ARTS STORY

I was sweet 16 and naive. The world beyond my wall of books was still a mystery. Irony at its finest, it was in the parking lot of my library, where my world finally opened.

It was an ordinary day in my hometown of Gallatin, TN. A special event day at the library where I volunteered, changed my life. By the end of the day, it was extraordinary.

Life is better in person. The film of the television screen hid the intensity of martial arts movies. I saw it in real life, on that life changing day. Dancing with Lightning, I called it. My eyes read the words "Ernie Reyes World Martial Arts." My ears heard the thundering music. My nose smelled a change in seasons. My lips smiled. My heart felt the beat.

My first love. My imagination had never dreamed up anything this good. My books were only a shadow of this intensity. This was real. This was really good.

I wanted it. I wanted to feel the way they looked. In the center of them all, stood a black belted man. Their star. The one whose flowing blonde hair only added to the flashiness of his moves.

His bright eyes caught mine watching. Our eyes met. I recognized something in him I'd never seen before. Be that as ironic as it reads. A flash, and it was gone. I couldn't name it. I still can't. But I know what it is.

I was in love. In love with everything I believed I wasn't but was somehow encapsulated in this thing called martial arts. The other half of me I wanted to be, but wasn't.

In them I saw bravery, confidence, power not meant for control, strength, and zeal.

Within me, I saw I was scared of the world outside my homeschooled walls. Insecure because I believed I as Leslie had nothing of value besides my long hair. Power I was used to in an overpowering form from the men in my life. I believed I was weak because I believed my body was broken. Excitement I had but not zeal. Zeal has a goal. I just had a feeling.

I wanted it. I wanted to be one of them. One of those people dancing with lightning.

Looking back, I can see my first step towards loving myself was taken there. I had found my other half. The barefooted road full of life's treasures I couldn't yet see, but I could feel. Diamonds my burning heart had yet to create. God had shown me the way. Money was the only thing standing in my way.

I began baby sitting and cleaning houses to pay for classes. Some afternoons, as the toilet flushed down the bleach, a few high and mighty tears, were washed away too.

"Am I really cleaning up other people's shit to pay for martial arts? Is it really worth it?" I asked myself. Not so deep down I knew it was.

Finally, I had a fistful of cash, ready to punch a bag. And I did. And it was fantastic.

Freshly washed gi, white belt untied because I didn't know how, a tummy full of butterflies, I met martial arts, the love of my life, feet to the mat.

I'll never forget walking onto that red carpet. Literally. It was bright red. Nearly as red as my nervously blushing cheeks. I had no idea what to do. But I knew I was in the right place. It already felt like home. The bright overhead lights reflected off a wall of mirrors. Above hung painted plaques stating their Student Creed, a Black Belt Success System, among other words of wisdom. A corner housed punching bags, pads, and weapons. People stretched, talked, and trained all around me. It felt like my new home.

Class began, though by which instructor I don't remember. Probably 5th degree Kwan Jang Nim (KJN) David Hughes. He was the older, wiser, leader of the school. The one whose stare made me question how much he saw, and how much he knew. I was totally intimidated, especially when I saw his biceps were bigger than my thighs.

His beautiful wife 3rd degree Sa Bum Nim (SBN) Sandy led the ladies' class. She was kind and had a warm smile. A toned body, and a confident walk that said she could kick any bad guy's butt.

Then there was the black belted man, 3rd degree Sa Bum Nim, (SBN) Allen Clark. He had it all. The confidence, the drive, the skills, the smile, the welcoming attitude, and so much more I can't even describe or name. He was the picture of who I wanted to be. I was starstruck. I've never seen a hero in real life, but he looked like one to me.

I loved, I lived. For a long time, Ernie Reyes World Martial Arts was the best part of my life. It will always feel like home to me. I began to "find myself" there.

One day, during class, I looked up and saw my reflection in the wall of mirrors. It was me. I was the girl, powerfully punching the bag. I was the one whose sore legs were still kicking. There was a burn in my chest that didn't hurt. It wasn't coming from crying, as it always had. I'd never even dared to punch a pillow. Yet there I was, learning how to defend myself against a bad guy. Pushing my body past what I thought it could do. Strengthening my heart both physically and emotionally. I smiled, at my reflection, as the tickles of pride began to introduce themselves to my feelings. A feeling I was unfamiliar with. I was doing something awesome. I felt awesome, for the first time in my life.

I felt frozen, the day I heard Allen say, "You remind me of myself." I was practicing my front kick in the front room, after class one day. I wanted an "A" on my belt test, so I trained, until the doors locked me out. Time would reveal that freezing is my body's natural response to both good and bad shock. This time, was really good. My heart did cartwheels in my chest. "My hero noticed me!" my heart squealed. Not only did he notice me, but it was one of the best moments of my life, where I felt, and I knew, I was in the right place, at the right time. I don't remember my reply. Probably something awkward and insecure, as I was at that time.

I trained on and off at Ernie Reyes for years, stopped only by the paper-thin wall of money. But I never gave up hope, and I never stopped training at home, and anywhere else I could. It's been 15 years, and I can still smell the fresh sweat. The white gis have faded from use. The belts have never been washed. Martial arts, I called it Dancing with Lightning. But it was more. So much more I had yet to see, and have yet to become.

Someday I will feel Allen Clark tie a Black Belt around my waist, not a day too late. That's the funny thing about dreams: they come true, but we never say they come too late. Mine is 16 years in the making. I know it will come true at the right time, and I know it will be the best moment of my life.

In between falling in love with Dancing with Lightning, and my dreams, is my story. But before my story is heard, you need to know his, first. The story of my hero, Allen Clark. My ending is better, when you know how his story starts.

4 ALLEN CLARK

The stage is set. It's the 1980's southern suburb, Gallatin, TN, where kids' baseballs in backyards flew faster than cars on the interstate. Kids played in the floorboards with their toys as seat belt laws weren't as firmly enforced. The whole world lived a little slower and more careful back in the good ole' days.

His family was loving and kind, doing the best with what they had. Never letting their girl, boy, boy, children want for anything, even a push. If one of their children put their minds to something, their mom and dad backed them, to the end. Failure was a part of life, dropping out was not.

In a time before participation awards, there existed only 1st, 2nd and 3rd place. Help and recognition were given only to those whose hands of life, came up a little short. Allen's sister, plagued by hearing problems at an early age, received classic southern hospitality as hands helped, and guided her through life. Allen, silently, watched and learned.

Sandwiched between the role of firstborn son, and the forgotten middle child, he smiled, at everyone, through the pressure. Unsure of where or who he was supposed to be, he longed to be recognized, for having something to show, not because of his role.

An accident brought him down. 9-years-old, he was playing with his toys on the floorboard behind the driver's seat. Left leg snugly placed between the front seat and the driver's door. Like a cat that fits wherever it sits. A 15mph metal clap awakened him.

He awoke to nothing but a memory of severe pain. 3 days had passed, lost to blackness covering the surgeries. Blackout curtain lifting to reveal his thigh to ankle cast.

He was 40 years old during my interview for this story. I asked him what the hardest part of it all was. He said it was here. When, at 9 years old, the most life changing words he had ever heard, came from the cold and unfamiliar voice of a stranger.

Had it been his loving mother, telling him he would never walk normally again, he told me it would have been easier to hear.

9 years old isn't really enough life for time to be comprehended. Still beginning his steps in life, he couldn't see the stages, a bum leg, would slow his walk through.

His father knew. In an act of extremely tough fatherly love, Allen Sr, gave Allen Jr, the greatest pep talk he ever heard.

"Do you believe what the doctors told you?" his father asked.

"I don't understand what it all means," 9-year-old Allen replied.

"I do, and I don't believe them. Get some good sleep tonight, son. Tomorrow we are going to work. Tomorrow it's going to begin to hurt. Tomorrow the Monday Night Football field, becomes your battleground. You are going to feel the worst pain you've ever felt. You are going to want to quit some days. You may even hate me for a time. But son, I promise you, in the end, it will be worth it."

What followed was years worth of a private life story between father and son. A story of change. A story of seeing one step beyond the pain. A story of a question, "Is the pain of one more leg lift, worse than staying here, staying the same?" Through tears, pain, and childhood angst, Allen lifted his leg, again, again, and again.

Try as she did, his loving mother could only hold his hand as the growing lukewarm and familiar voices rinsed and repeated the risks before every reconstructive surgery. Eventually, the doctors stopped telling him what he already knew. He learned he was in for an uphill battle with a bum leg.

Eventually there came a day, when the pain, became strength. The pain had faded, giving Allen sight to the goal his father saw. His lifts became higher. His leg became stronger. He began to walk, then run, past his father's goals, to Gallatin's rite of passage for boys: sports.

Minor league baseball gave him a game he could get good at, but also a team he could hide behind. Hiding his bum leg behind a smile, he played his own game. He could catch, standing still, thus left became his field. Running, he passed to other players. He never told anyone his secret.

Painful growth reconstructive surgeries through the years put his life on pause, which he grew tired of. At 14, he told the doctors, "Just give me a knee." Move on and move up was in his line of sight. Get the bum leg off the To-Do List.

After the last surgery, his feet found a skateboard. His bum leg leading as his strong one propelled behind him. Unbeknownst to him, skateboarding fundamentals trained a foundation in him even his bum leg couldn't shake: balance.

Beginning as an ordinary rainy day, his life found the way, to extraordinary. While riding his skateboard through a bowling alley parking lot, a sign appeared in the corner: "$19.95 Trial Program." His pocket held a rainy day $20. The trial was for martial arts. His life was about to find its footing.

Hiding his bum leg behind the loose fabric of the gi, he trained. Limitations he fought with faked confusion. His leg couldn't stretch so his mind had to. If he knew he couldn't fit the movement's mold, he broke the mold by faking awkward. Awkward was better than an asterisk by his name. No pity podium for Allen.

At 15 his bum leg found its stability. The same bike that rode him to the martial arts studio's door, rode the waves of growth, one cold day with his friends. Overworked and out of breath, he dismounted. For the first time ever, he limped in front of his friends. A warm and friendly, "You ok?" cold-cocked him to the big picture. "Yeah, why?" he said as he straightened. He mastered his outward expression of pain that day, never again to limp in front of his friends. The whole world became his training ground.

With a smile on his face, he trained, and laughed like the Joker, at the card he had been dealt.

2 years into martial arts, his game of hide and sneak was called out. In an attempt to bring the next level out in Allen, his own instructor, KJN David, punched a combination of buttons, within him. It worked. Challenged to fight a student who fought by the book, David told him he couldn't beat the student.

Flashback to the doctor who said he couldn't walk. Where someone else said "couldn't" Allen heard a "challenge."

Allen accepted the match within the rules set: Allen could use his arsenal of movements; the student could only use his left hand. A slap in the face of the martial arts world. Allen's fire burned. This time, his leg wasn't bum anymore, and he was ready to fight.

His mask stayed on the first round, not wanting to hurt the student, but still giving him a match worthy of a fight-back.

Allen's honor began cracking his mask, in round 2. The victory smile on the student's face was paid for with a lie. A lie Allen was telling him, by holding back. The mask came off in the name of honor and truth, a gift for both young men.

The shot heard round the studio was that of a sidekick pulled 1 inch from the student's head. His bum leg, now holding him up. The clock dinged, jaws dropped, and the mask was written into Allen's history.

"What was that?" KJN David wrote onto the new chapter of Allen's life.

"That was me."

He went on to win the international competition of AAA Championship title, before becoming a regional champion. Literally meaning he won the world of martial arts before winning his home country. Not only did he win the title, he won it at Red Belt, a feat never before accomplished by anyone other than a Black Belt.

6 months later, and 6 months earlier than most, he tied his Black Belt around his waist.

Pride glowed in the eyes of his childhood surgeon who came to watch the ceremony. Glow reflecting off the x-rays he had brought per Allen's request; they smiled together. KJN David spotted and stopped.

As David's eyes wandered over the x-rays, questions, ran across his face. "This is the man who gave me my knee," Allen said. The truth was finally free.

Allen's Joker card had been turned and burned to reveal an Ace. Standing strong, supported by his knee, he stood alone in the spotlight of his victory.

Years, later, when life's little lessons had put a gap in Allen's mind, it was his not so little brother, DJ, who filled it in.

"I just don't want to be alone anymore," Allen said.

"You're not alone," DJ said, "I'm right here with you, in Gallatin, TN."

I asked him, at the end of this interview, what his proudest moment in martial arts was in his past. He looked me dead-set in the eyes, and said, "Be here now, and enjoy it."

5 SECRET SHAME

I never thought I would ever be writing this story. Years ago, had you told me I would be typing my shame story for the whole world to read, I probably would have rudely laughed in your face. Laughter hiding the terror beating my heart. But here I am, still unsure if these words are the right ones to write. I have written, I have cried, I have called my mom and told her I still don't understand why. It still hurts. It still burns. It's the one happy ending, even I can't find.

But here it is, for all the world to read. It has to be told, as it's integral to my story. These are the hardest, scariest, worst words I've ever expressed.

I never stopped wetting the bed at night.

Before I let my feelings takeover my heart and my head, I've decided I'm just going to give you the facts. That's all that really matters anyway. I don't want you to feel my pain. I don't want you to feel my shame. Why would I? It's the worst part of my life. It's unfair and downright rude, to put all of that on you. So, I'm going to erase the sob story I have written down, and just tell you what you need to know for now. It will be raw and probably won't be prettily worded, but it's the truth.

After exhausting all at home methods, at 12-years old, my parents took me to a specialist, who ran a gamut of tests. No answers were found. My body was normal, even though I saw it as broken.

Sleepovers and church retreats, I mostly stayed home from. The maintenance required, to my young self, just wasn't worth it. Nor was the cost.

Why didn't I chance the gamble? Because I was terrified of my friends finding out. At 12-years-old I told 2 of my friends. A chorus of "Eww!" was the reply to my confession. They never spoke to me again.

At church the same judgement I heard with different words. Girls gossiping about an outfit worn by one girl, too many times in a month. Weeks of whispered questions asking if another was pregnant. I listened and learned, the worst of condemnations from the mouths in church. Faster than you could change your clothes, or your mind, people were ostracized.

I was in high school, when I learned, church people, are the same people as me buying detergent at the store. The only difference is church people like to hide their dirty laundry behind Sunday's best dress. I felt it best, that my pee stained laundry, was left hidden.

Every winter I had diaper rash. Every step burned my ass, every year. I learned how to hide pain, with a fake smile on my face.

Waking up in my own piss, day after day, was shitty. I felt unclean and unfairly hurt. Add the blood of womanhood, and my sheets often looked like a movie murder scene. Every morning I had a mess to clean. Every night I could smell my own pee. It wasn't worth my time to change my sheets, every single day. I began every morning on defense, ducking and covering until the shower made me fit to join humanity. That's how I felt.

I just wanted to know why. What lesson was God trying to teach me? Where was the good in my pain? Where is the happy ending? Night after night I cried and prayed. Begged God for answers. None came. I began to cuss at Him, once I learned what those words were. Yes, the words "Fuck You God!" came out of my mouth, and broken heart. I'm not proud of it, but it's the truth.

I clung to Jesus, those solo pity party nights. I imagined as vividly as I could, my pillow was Jesus' lap. I imagined His Hand brushing my hair and tears off my cheeks. I imagined the words He would say, answers, that never came. Well, to be fair, maybe the answers did come, but I was too focused on my own pain to listen. I cried, cuddled, and cussed while He cuddled and comforted me. It might sound crazy, but it's the truth.

In the morning, in the shower, sometimes tears and water would flow. Soft and warm pillow replaced by the cold and firm shower wall. I'd imagine it was Jesus' chest. The streams of warm water flowing over me, were His strong arms, holding me. Holding me up, as the soap and suds, washed my shame down the drain. Knowing the very next morning, life would be the same.

Maybe I am weak, maybe I'm a wimp, for crying all those years, like I did. Maybe, it's balance.

In my 20's the bar scene began, ending always with my excuses to return home, no matter how drunk I was.

Yes, I shamefully admit, I drove home drunk, night after night, believing the cost of sharing my secret shame, cost less than a

DUI. I could have packed a bag; I could have taken a chance. But after losing childhood friends to my truth, I just couldn't do it. I had lived and I had learned. It had hurt, it just wasn't worth it.

By God's grace, He kept myself, and all the other drivers safe. I know I was scared, selfish, and stupid.

Questions I'm not sure I want the answer to, began to invade my dreams of the future. My Southern Belle American Dream was founded on black and white tile, a pink fridge, a husband and babies to love.

With that dream, came a nightmare. Questions I didn't want to have to face, and decisions, I didn't want to have to make. When my crying baby awoke to be fed, and I was wet, what was I supposed to do? Sit there, in my own wet diaper, both of us, in my stench? Shower off while my baby cried so we could be comfortable? Change my own diaper, odor still there, a halfway point, to be fair? No matter what I chose, someone is crying. My hungry baby, or a feeling like a failure, mommy, me.

Either way, as it seems, instead of raising a family, God wanted me to raise my wings.

Everything changed, during the night, the day Prince Charming walked into my life.

Within hours I was falling in love, within hours I was brave enough. My secret shame was laid before his ears and mind. I waited, tears flowing from my eyes. To my surprise, he accepted me, and my shame, into his arms, that night.

In the wake of morning light, to my surprise, I was dry. I chalked it up to luck. Luck doesn't last for very long, but this did. Every night I was in his arms, my diaper stayed dry. It was my sign. It was the "yes" my fairytale, I believed. I fell in love hard and fast.

It's fair to ask if I would have fallen in love with my Prince had my cure not occurred. Yes, I would have. I was in love with him. Down my "Future Husband Questions Checklist" we went, up went my hopes, not a single answer he gave was wrong.

5 months after meeting, we rode off into the afternoon in a big white van, holding hands. Hometown was Nashville, my home was now the mountains.

Hopeful but skeptical, it took me months before I became brave enough to not wear a diaper to bed.

I'll never forget the night, when, for the first time in my life, I wore my favorite teacup pajama pants, a pink tank top, and slid beneath the covers, diaper free. No crinkle of the waterproof bed pad could be heard. No padded barrier keeping me away from him. I was finally free. I cried happy tears. He nearly did too.

I slept, wrapped in the warmth of his strong arms. Blissfully happy, happier than I knew I could be. Morning came, the brightest sun I'd ever seen, the brightest smile I'd ever worn. My Prince was still asleep. I wallowed. I wallowed in the warmth, the cleanliness, the calm, the new choice I got to make: Where do I go from here? Instead of ducking and covering to the bathroom, I got to choose. It's the little things.

I stood up straight, smiling. I got up slowly, savoring each new barefooted step. I walked. I walked past the bathroom. I smiled. I'd never done that before.

"This is what mornings are supposed to feel like," my heart said.

"I love seeing you smile," God said.

"This new beginning, is your new history," my mind said.

So, what does a woman do the morning of what feels like her first day of freedom? Coffee, of course. Steaming cup in hand, I walked back to bed. I'd never done that before either.

For the first time in my life, I got back in bed, still wearing the same, still clean, pink pajamas. I slid into the still clean sheets, next to my adorable sleeping Prince Charming.

"Thank you Jesus!" my heart cried.

"You're welcome darling," He said.

"I love this new chapter," my mind sighed.

The next 3 years I spent blissfully diaper free. My first morning thought often being a "Thank You Jesus!" prayer. Then coffee. Every morning, instead of living on defense, I simply lived, and smiled.

As my love goggles began to crack, and our love story began its final countdown, my nighttime nightmare, came back. It began early in the year, a wet night there, a wet night here. Until, by July 4th, our love story's end, it was back again.

I could insert a myriad of metaphors here to describe how I felt there, but I see no point. If you've ever lost a love, gotten dizzy and sick from the unknown direction life was going in, or been hurt by something you deemed unfair, you understand my feelings. It fucking sucked. I was crying and cussing God again. This is the one happy ending, even I can't find. But I know I will. Somewhere on this side of the rainbow

6 SIDES TO MY LOVE LIFE

Capital Letter

Once Upon a Time, it began on bended knee. Prince Charming waltzed through my apartment door, knelt, and introduced himself to me. I pinky promise he did. After weeks of texting, hundreds of miles of a trip he finally made, and there we were, finally, face to face. He, on bended knee, and myself, already imagining him holding a ring.

He was cuter than his pictures. So much cuter. He knelt, his eyes staring curiously, excitedly, nervously, into mine. He held out his hand. Time seemed to slow as I slid mine into his. He brought my hand to his lips, and as though we were in a movie, he gently kissed it.

"*This is how Happily Ever After begins,*" my heart sighed.

"It's nice to meet you," he said.

"*All that glitters is not gold,*" my mind argued.

Head over heels and my heart I fell. Too good to be true, was actually happening. Add in my bedwetting stopping, and I thought myself a fool, if I refused.

We fast forwarded our love story. 5 months passed in time and Nashville I was already leaving behind. Far too fast for truth to be seen. That's the funny thing, about fast love stories: we only have time for words, the truth gets lost in the blur. The truth is seen, behind the scenes. That's why they say time will tell: time allows for rinse and repeat. It's when the scene plays out again, the first impression mask, cracks. Time after time, layer after layer, until what we know, are the bare bones. Truth doesn't require a yes or no. It simply, is. I never gave us time for that. I was too busy looking for the signs, I missed the red flags.

Comma

His loving mama taught him well. "Always bring her flowers, even if it's a wild flower. It will make her smile for hours." On their rolling farmland he ran, bringing his sweet mama flowers in his hands. She smiled, he smiled. I smiled when he did the same for me. Grocery stores replaced the rolling hills. And, much to my thrill, rarely did his hands hold only one bouquet. Three or four would often frame his excited face.

"I'd rather have roses on my table than diamonds on my neck," Emma Goldman said. I agree. Every Sunday when I was single, a bouquet for my living room I would buy. Sometimes more, if the price was right. The room seemed to glow with life, if flowers were in sight. It was my way of loving on myself.

****

He once brought me a single red rose to work. I held it, smelled it, and smiled. "Why don't you look inside it?" he asked, and grinned a grin he wore when he was up to something sweet. Slowly, so as not to tear the featherweight petals, I pushed aside the velvet pages. Sparkles. Sparkles and rainbows. Nested in the center, an opal rested in silver. My birthstone. I grinned.

"This is what love stories are written with," my heart sighed.

"I hope you like it," Prince Charming smiled.

"Girl keep him!" my coworker exclaimed.

"If he does it once he will do it again, if he means it," my mind meddled.

***

It was nearly Golden Hour, as we drove the back-way home from town in my little red car. Fall was trickling in, teasing the edges of leaves with a honey glow. Some trees had already abandoned their green leaves and gone yellow, swaying like giant dandelions over the mountains we drove through. The black road curled like a ribbon around the mountains. My little red car looked like a little red ladybug, playing hide and seek with the sun's beams. Prince Charming was driving, I was daydreaming.

The car began to slow, to the side of the road he drove. I looked over to see, one of my favorite smiles on his face. He was up to something sweet. I smiled. He loved me. His eyes were set on something I didn't see. Prince Charming, parked, and sprang from his seat.

Out of the car he left, and up the mountain he ran, climbing it like it was an anthill made of sand. Farm boys, from the outside, their strength you rarely see, until the moment comes, farm boys, turn into Hercules. So sexy. Prince Charming was strong. Even when I weighed over 200lbs, he could easily lift me off the ground.

His long arms scooped up yellow daisies I could now see dotting the mountainside. I nearly cried.

"This is love, and this is my real life," my heart burst.

"These are for you my Bride!" he panted excitedly.

"This smells funny," my mind mused.

I buried my smiling self into the yellow pillow and inhaled. It smelled like shit. True story. His eyes, once bright a moment ago, now crinkled, in disgust.

"Did you fart?" We asked simultaneously. "No!" We echoed.

Our eyes fell on the flowers as our minds recognized the smell: from a skunk's butt.

My next breath I breathed in so much of that dank odor, and burst out into hysterical laughter.

"This is what tears of joy are made of," my heart laughed along.

"I am so sorry baby!" he said, his face turning red.

"It's the thought that counts," my mind giggled.

Out the window went the flowers and into the back of my car he dug. He knew I kept wipes for such times. He bashfully and carefully wiped my hands and face as my laughter poured from my lips. He was so embarrassed. His face was red as a sunburn. In between giggles I tried to speak words.

"It was a wonderful thought darling, thank you for trying." "I'll get you more the next time we go to town," he mumbled beneath reddened cheeks.

Good golly miss Molly he was cute. It was times like this, I held onto. When he smiled like a schoolboy with a crush. When his eyes glinted oh so mischievous. It was in these moments, I felt his love.

For 3.5 years it rained flowers on me like a falling rainbow. I was spoiled expectant and he always delivered. Even when he was mad at me, he still brought them home. I loved him even more then. He loved me. The flowers told me so.

Oxford Comma

He would always take me somewhere beautiful and during my dating visits to the mountains to see him. I fell in love with the earth then. Snowcapped mountains, glimmering waterfalls, caves, and mud for days. We played and explored the world together. Love was blooming. Until we shared the same home, then everything changed.

When he had me there in the mountains, he didn't seem to want to spend time with me anymore. Retrospect told me he didn't want me, he just wanted something better than what he had: loneliness. Instead of weekend adventures, his world was video games. He was my world, so I stayed by his side.

Work kept him later into the night, over the years. The mountains kept his cell from getting signal. From dusk till dawn his signal was as spotty as a Dalmatian puppy, he said. Some nights he never came home. Fell asleep in his car on the side of the road, he said. I believed him. But I knew better.

I knew I had tagged along on his work routes, and saw my cell bars go down. But I also knew I had been warned. Not so deep down I knew why he wasn't coming home. Proved true when, in the months before our ending, I snooped through his phone. I wish I could erase those words from my memory. Ignorance would have been bliss.

Ellipsis

They say the road to hell is paved with good intentions. Ladies, I am exhibit A. I cheated, because I loved him.

"Oh no she didn't," I can hear you say. Yes, yes, I did. True story. And I'm not sure I feel "bad enough" for doing it. I just didn't know what else to do.

I couldn't see the bruises, when the bedroom lights were low, but I could feel them, and I could remember them.

Their stories played behind my eyes, getting in the way of our love. My mind and heart played a vicious game of tug of war.

"*How can his hands do both?*" my heart and mind begged to know.

"*Love doesn't do this,*" they echoed.

Closing my eyes, I saw the memories play. Open, I saw a face that had smiled, smirked, and snarled.

For nearly two years I fought my secret battle. Trying to live and love in the moment. Trying to find the best in him, in us.

As long as we could make love, our love, I believed, would be alright. Call me weak minded, for being unable to keep the memories away. It won't change a thing. At least I fought, at least I tried. Eventually there were too many memories, and I wanted to cry. I prayed for a miracle. My Prince gave me a weed.

I'd tried it a few times before. Never liked it. It made my mind too busy. He said maybe being in this safe environment at home would make it better. It was not safe, but it was how My Beast played his game. I nearly puked from coughing so hard. He laughed.

As the smoke left my lungs, along with it went my worries. My head began to clear. It felt like the walls of protection I had built within my head and heart, were tumbling down. I felt more love towards him, less fear. I liked it. I loved him more.

I'd heard veterans used marijuana for PTSD, I then understood why. When you see the sharp edges of life, a little sugar coating, truly helps. Weed helped my mind like a helping hand. Its leaves even looked like one to me. Senses heightening, I asked if we could go to the bedroom.

For the first time since the blood and bruises had begun, it was just us, in my mind and in the bedroom. No memories to fight, no pain seeping in, no bullshit. It was a miracle.

For the next 1.5 years I can count on 2 hands the number of times we had sex that I wasn't high. I told him I liked how it heightened my senses. True, but I liked how it relaxed my mind more.

In the last 6 months, there were too many memories for the smoke to hide. My mind began battling again. I fought it, hard. But I had to face reality through the puffs of powdered-sugar-coated smoke.

The reality was that I missed making love with my Prince, without all the extra bullshit. The bad memories, the weed filter, and the constant questioning of how his hands could do both. Love doesn't do that. I missed the early days when we were young, and wild and free. But that was over then. I missed him. If we couldn't make love, and be together, what did we really have? It felt both broken and fake. I wanted something real. So I went out and found it.

I found someone with whom I was comfortable, but had no chemistry, and I slept with him. I wanted to see what it felt like to be touched by a man whose hands I wasn't afraid of. Rightfully so, it blew up in my face. People always hide their ugly sides when the lights are on.

I wish I could tell you I got some grand epiphany, a one size fits all answer, or at least a lesson learned. But honestly, I can't. I did learn some things about myself, but not how to fix us. I had cheated on love, in order to try and save, that very love. I had broken the heart. Regardless of the fact, I knew he already had. Was I right? Was I wrong? Only God can judge me, they say. So, can I.

I learned I wish I felt more guilty, than I do. Even years later, to this very day. I don't feel as bad as I think I should. What the heck does that mean about me? I wish there had been another way. But all my prayers, all the things I changed, all the violence I forgave, couldn't put our love back together again. I saw no other way.

My guilty conscience convinced me to admit what I had done. I came clean 2 weeks after he broke up with me. I was still hoping, foolishly, we would get back together someday. I didn't want that confession to wait. My daydreams had spun a tale of change, growing on our own for a year, coming back together at the end. I knew I'd have to tell him then. Better for him to know now so he could make a fully informed decision then.

My conscience became clear, but it didn't feel like I had done the right thing. Retrospect says I shouldn't have told. Retrospect also wants to deny the smile on his face he tried to hide. He smiled at some of the most inopportune times. I never understood why.

But I did have a clue. Months later I found out his story had changed from him leaving me because I was a drunk, to because I was a cheat. He was lying, and I was crying.

Period

On July 4th, our love story ended. He came home, and said those 4 bad words.

"We need to talk."

I wanted to talk to him too, about my latest and greatest epiphany. This time was different. This time I knew.

"*How many times have you said that before?*" my mind recounted.

"*It only takes one,*" my heart replied.

I'd spent the day cleaning and praying. Praying for an answer, a miracle, anything.

I didn't want to give up on love. If we could conquer this, we could conquer anything, it seemed, or so I believed. I desperately wanted love to win. He had it in him. I saw the potential. I believed in love and I believed in him.

Eventually I felt God, I'm unsure of how to word it, I guess, resign to my decision to fight through. I felt Him back off. He wanted me to leave, I knew. But I wanted to stay and win one for love. I felt a shift in the echoes of my prayers. Then my answer came.

"*Listen to his sad songs, Leslie. He's trying to tell you something,*" God said. "*There's step 1.*"

With renewed love and vigor, I eagerly waited for him to come home so I could tell him my latest and greatest epiphany. This time it would work. This time was different. I just knew it. The back door opened, I was grinning, he wasn't. I was eager and hopeful. He had a look on his face I'd never seen before. It didn't look good, but I ignored it.

"I have something to tell you!" I said, excitedly.

He said the 4 bad words.

"We need to talk."

I don't need to tell you the words of what happened next. I see no good coming from such sadness. Most women have been there, lived that. Suffice to say he left me because I was a drunk. Sad but too true. I couldn't argue. My heart was broken but I had no one to blame but myself.

Feelings and emotions exploded like popcorn in the tornado my life had just become.

Relief said, "At least you survived. Now you have a second chance at love and happiness."

Despair said, "They were wrong when they said it's better to have loved and lost."

Heartache said, "This wasn't ever supposed to happen again."

Grief said, "No one will ever be able to replace him."

Nostalgia said, "Maybe you'll look back on these as the good ole days."

My brain said, "Bullshit."

The Princess in me asked, "Am I still a Princess?"

Jesus said, "Yes."

The dreamer in me said, "Leslie, you were living a nightmare, there are far better days ahead."

The little girl in me whined, "But the bed will be cold and lonely again."

"Hug your pillow and imagine its Jesus again," she replied.

Love, put the exclamation point on the end.

Question Mark

Brokenhearted, I decided to stay in my beloved mountains. My heart had found a happy place in the sparkling white snow Nashville rarely received. I loved driving through white tippy-topped mountains. Walking up and over white-caked topped peaks. Stopping to see, forests blanketed in snow so glittery and sparkly. My heart could breathe, beat, and be. I found peace within the white winter wonderland. Sadly, my wallet didn't care what my heart wanted.

I don't remember the moment I was reminded of my beloved martial arts. Or when the image of my hero, Allen Clark put stars back into my eyes. Or when I decided to write my life into this book.

I do remember, sitting on my couch, smoking a bowl in one hand, laptop in my lap, mapping out my life's possibilities, for weeks. I remember tracking Allen down, finding him listed as a coach at a gym back home near Nashville, TN, and feeling the tickles of hope, through my heartache. Wondering, if I could actually do it. If I would, actually do it. If I should, do it.

Could I start over, restarting back at my home plate? In my heart's happy place. Would I be able to fight back, through the memories and the PTSD, and find the joy, martial arts gave me? Is this the path I should choose? Or was I a fool? Was there something better for me to do?

My heart ached for martial arts since leaving that red carpeted floor. I yearned to feel all those feel-goods again. All those feelings that filled the empty places in my heart like no man ever had. I felt whole and complete; I felt like me. I missed that Leslie, and I missed my hero Allen. He made me feel like I could be whoever I wanted to be.

I remember still seeing stars around Allen's face. Soon clouded by paternalistic disappointment saying, "You knew better than that," I imagined I would hear after I told him I didn't use anything he taught me. The image of looking up to my hero, and him looking down at me, stung in my dreams. But I had to tell him the truth. For a reason I can't remember, I wanted him to know what had happened, even if no one else ever did.

"I want this more than anything," my heart confessed.

"I think this is a very good choice," my mind decided.

My lips spoke the three-letter word that changes life, I said "Yes.

7 DECEMBERS DANCING

December 1st
The Open Door
Dear Diary,

I've been here before, a long time ago in a life far far away: the parking lot of my beloved martial arts.

I was 16 then, I'm 30 now. I was naive then; I know better now.

Ahead I can see my barefooted road, at least a few steps ahead. Up to the doorway of the gym my hero, Allen Clark, now runs. I can barely see him through the glimmering glass in front of me. I can't wait to see him. He is everything I want to be. Now, I'm here, coming home, to train and fight to become the best, me, while under his wing. I don't know how to get there, but he will. He always knows. I'm so glad I'm here now.

I wonder if it will feel the same. My love of martial arts. I remember the rush; I remember the freedom. Wait, that's silly. I know I've changed; it can't feel the same. My eyes now know what the bad guy looks like.

Maybe it's silly of me to think I can do this. Though I'm not exactly sure what this is. I do know I want to fight back against my PTSD. Sitting and talking in therapy isn't enough for me. I want to do something.

I know I want Allen to put me back in my worst fears, the worst of what my Beast did to me. But this time I want to and will defend myself. I know I want to punch a picture of a bruise until it tears in two. I want to not be so afraid. I want to fight for my own happy ending.

It's been 10 years since my feet left that red carpet. 10 years of training on my own time, in my own ways. Never giving up that feeling, of my best days, of my best me.

My hands trembled in excitement as I pulled open the gym door. I walked in grinning. As my feet stepped over the threshold, I heard my hero's voice. 30 years old and I'm still starstruck. Some things never change. I hope this never does.

"Wow!" Allen said.

"I'm so happy to be home!" my heart exclaimed.

"Once Upon a Time," my mind said.

He was in the "ring" I think they call it. He and a pretty young girl both held swords. His eyes held surprise, curiosity, and a dash of what looked like amusement. My eyes took it all in.

Grin deepening, I stated the obvious, 'It's been a while."

He laughed, "Well yeah it has."

"We have a lot to talk about when you're done," I said, knowing manners mattered.

As he continued his lesson with the girl, I wandered around the first day of the next chapter of my life.

White walls climbed what looked nearly two stories high. A red halo wrapped around midway high. Words reading "Strength," "Perseverance," "Determination," "Hard Work," among other words that help make you go, painted white words within the halo. The list wrote all the way around the gym. To my left, the front door and desk. Treadmills and I think they are called elliptical machines, lined the rest of the windowed wall. Like jellyfish legs, black body bags swayed beneath red bars on the left half of the gym. Black and red soundproofing foam squares checkerboarded the far-left wall behind them, above a green runway of flooring between the wall and the bags. Giant mirrors gleamed on the wall opposite the windows.

In front of me was open black flooring. On the far wall, bathrooms, banners, and bulletin boards checkered the white wall. On the floor between, silver machines I have no clue the names of, stood. One of the machines looked like it's for pull-ups. Bucket list. I've never been able to do one. *"By summer I will,"* I pinky promised myself.

In the far-right corner were more machines and weights. Big ones. I have no idea what the big machines are used for or called. The only thing I recognized were dumbbells and kettlebells lining the side wall beneath more gleaming mirrors.

To my immediate right, the ring stood atop black steps and cubby holes. White wire walled around the black mat, where Allen and the girl stood. I sat on the couch between the ring and the front door, and watched.

A few minutes later, Allen's hello hug, welcomed me home. Grinning in surprise, he asked, "How are you?!"

"Much better now that I'm here. It's so good to see you. We have lots to talk about."

"Oh yeah?" "Yeah. We may not get to it all today."

"Let's talk after boxing class. Do you have gloves?"

I showed him my karate gloves I'd kept since my high school Ernie Reyes days.

"Those will work for now but you need to get boxing gloves soon. Class starts in 15, you can warm up on the green." Smiling, I walked to the green runway beneath the checkerboarded wall.

As I stretched, people began to arrive. Allen walked over, and the class started.

It was odd seeing him like this. In a new place, no gi, no red carpet or 3rd degree Black Belt to be seen. I wondered what degree he is now.

It all came back, in a flood of happy flashbacks.

Time seemed to slow as my hands slipped into the gloves. My bare feet took my unorthodox fighting stance, left leg back.

My fists clenched in my gloves; my eyes saw the black body bag target. My ears heard the words "jab" "cross" "uppercut." My feet felt my stance change my angle as I moved. I punched. My fists felt the impact of the bag at the end of my gloves. My heart swelled in strength, reminded of the best parts of me, I forgot I had within myself.

"I'm right where I'm meant to be," my heart said.

"Add left roundhouse, right roundhouse," Allen said.

"This is one of the smartest decisions you've ever made Leslie," my mind said.

Muscle memory flooded my mind and body. It was all coming back to me. I welcomed it with clenched fists.

My heart stirred and swirled. I love this. I love martial arts. It makes me feel and believe I can be everything I think I'm not. It fills in the missing parts of Leslie. I love the fire that doesn't hurt. The intensity that doesn't burn. I love the strength not used for overpowering. I love the dynamite explosions of giving everything I have. I love the play fighting without hurting anyone, sparring, I think it's called. I love being in control of my growth. I love knowing 1000 punches thrown is 1000 times better. Second only to God, martial arts is the best decision I ever made. I've missed this so much.

Too soon it's over and I'm already counting down the hours until the next class.

As the gym emptied, the pages of my story opened.

In as few words as possible, I told Allen as much as I could.

"He put me in positions you taught me how to defend, Allen, but I didn't. I didn't defend myself," I said as tears filled my eyes.

"Why not Leslie?"

"I loved him, and love doesn't do that. An eye for an eye we both goes blind. Turn the other cheek. You don't fight fire with fire." The excuses poured from my lips like poison.

"That's not how those words and Bible verses are meant. You know that."

I hung my head. "I do now. Back then I just tried to pray my way out of it. I begged God to pull a miracle. To be strong where I couldn't."

"How well did that work out for you?"

I shrugged, "I survived," I said. "He left after calling me a drunk, which I was. I hid the pain of my reality behind the blur of intoxication. Life was better there."

"Did you ever defend yourself?"

"Only when I was drunk, which was arguably too often. I was ok when I met him, but soon fell back into alcoholism when I moved in with him. My new life brought back old demons. I got bad back into drinking. But the liquid courage made me brave-ish. I defended myself a few times. Though I quickly learned defending myself, fueled him. He fed off my energy. I was safer submitting. He stopped sooner. I didn't know what to do. It was a lose-lose situation."

Allen's eyes held what looked like the paternalistic disappointment I knew was coming. But they held something else too, though I don't know what it was.

"Why are you here?" Allen asked.

"I never want to feel that way again. I want to fight back against my PTSD. Will you help me?"

Spoiler alert, Allen said, "Yes."

12.2

Smart As

Dear Diary,

I thought I was smarter than that. Smart enough to see the red flags. Smart enough to see the patterns. Smart enough to defend myself.

Problem is, I was. I'd watched crime dramas. I'd studied body language and people for years for fun. I even had the martial arts training.

I'm not one of those women who can claim she didn't know. I did know. I knew exactly how to get out of a choke. It was a white belt basic defence at Ernie Reyes World Martial Arts. As were other common attacks like a bear hug, tackle, haymaker, and headlock. I knew. My mind knew the moves, my muscles had drilled the defense. I just refused to use it when the time came.

I don't remember there ever being a moment in my high school training days where I imagined a familiar face on my attacker. It was always a masked mugger in the streets. Someone I didn't care about or love. An enemy.

All of them, I knew. One I was in love with, one I loved as a father figure, with one I was a prodigy, another there was a bit of chemistry, another was family. Connection changed my mind. I don't know why.

I do know I made the wrong choice. I could have done it. I would have been doing the right thing. I should have defended myself. All those times. But I never learned. Because I loved. Because I loved them more than myself. Because I didn't want to physically hurt them. Because I knew I could forgive them. Because, because, because, bullshit. Because I took Bible verses about forgiveness and sins being wiped away, too literally. Because I believed by giving them a clean slate, I was creating change. Because, in a way, I believe, I loved, the wrong way. If that's even possible.

My mind and heart seemed always at war with what love is and what love does. My mind said yes to defending myself. My heart said no. My body wanted to.

Maybe if I had loved them a little less, and myself a little more, I would have.

12.3
My Mask
Dear Diary,

I thought I was good at hiding what was going on until my cashier friends started asking questions. Never one to meet a stranger, I make cashiers my friends. Life is more fun that way. Grocery stores, the bank and soft blanket stores, everywhere I go.

Amanda asked. I told her I fell down, in a myriad of ways. Again, and again, I told her that.

She didn't believe me, after a while, none of them did. It wasn't long before I ran out of lies.

I got smart. A job in disaster restoration was the perfect hideaway. Nobody questioned my bruises anymore. I was safe.

I thought that by telling him I didn't want the police interfering he would feel lucky and be motivated to change. The bruises got bigger after that. I should have known. I did know. I just didn't want to believe it was happening, to me, or I was that naive.

12.5
Ring Around the Dragon
Dear Diary,

I saw it. Sitting on the couch, watching a class in the ring, I saw it. I saw my battleground. It's called Jiu Jitsu. That's how he did it. I saw them doing things Beast used to do to me. I wanted to cry. I couldn't cry, because there were people around the couch

I was sitting on. Fear and memories flooded my veins and mind as I watched.

"*No!*" my heart cried.

"The best way to get out of a position you don't like is to never get there in the first place," Allen's voice instructed. "If you do get there, you have to learn how to stay calm. You can't make clear decisions clouded with emotions."

"*Leslie, meet your dragon,*" my mind announced.

12.6

In with the Renewed

Dear Diary,

A week in and I've found my groove. I'm taking a circuit training class to get me to the finish line of my fitness goals. 50lbs down from the 207 I topped at. Boxing and kickboxing classes as long as my body can take it. I'm not ready for Jiu Jitsu.

I was a size 10 when I moved in with him. When things got bad, I felt sad so I ate my feelings. Within the 3 years I went from 145lbs to 207lbs. A size 10 to 18, I think. Not entirely sure on the size as I stopped wearing anything but stretchy clothes because muffin top became uncomfortable. Along with the extra fat came cushion: the violence hurt less.

Before our last holidays together, I hit my breaking point on being fat. I'll spare you the TMI details. Suffice to say my fat was getting in the way of normal human functions. I was having to shift it around to be able to do daily things. Just before the holidays, I hit another roadblock I had to shift my fat around. I decided right then and there to start exercising. Then my first roadblock came when I looked at the calendar. The holiday goody-goodies were coming up. I decided to start in January.

30lbs down the first year via workout videos. One job in disaster restoration later, I was down another 30. Life slowed and my weight yo-yo-ed. I began the circuit training class weighing in at 165. I don't know what my weight goal is. But I know what I want to look like. Between the circuit training, boxing and kickboxing classes, I'll get there someday.

For now, I'm taking it one pound, one punch, one barefooted step at a time.

"This feels good," my heart said.

"Drop and give me 10 burpees," Allen said.

"You can do it!" my mind said.

"You've got to be kidding me," I said.

12.7
Bad Mad

Dear Diary,

I'm not even mad at my Prince Charming. Though maybe I should be. I don't let myself get mad. I keep my pain simmering in sadness. It's safer there.

I've seen what anger does to people. Red faces, fingers pointing, people crying, constant battling. In the end someone always gets hurt and the winner wins because they beat someone down. Where is the happy in that?

I've only ever been mad at God and myself. Because He won't tell me the happy ending to my bedwetting. I wish I didn't feel that way, but it's true.

"Anger is a mentality," Allen said. "What you are feeling is not what is happening."

He's right. Sadness makes me want to cry, which I do, a lot. I wallow, waiting for the tears to end. Anger, I have no idea what to do with.

Maybe if I had gotten mad at my Beast, I would have defended myself, like Jesus did when He turned the tables in His temple when He found out it was being used as a marketplace. The temple was being abused and taken advantage of, like I was. Even He got mad and did what needed to be done. Even Jesus knew when words were not enough.

My body was like that temple. Purple, brown, green, yellow, red and colors I can't name, turned my body from a treasure chest, to a busted bank vault. Though I don't know what Beast got out of it. Not sure I want to know.

Some days I'd play out a fantasy of Jesus literally showing up at our door, on a white horse, to save me. Off into the sunset we would ride. The pretty picture made me smile.

12.8
My Place
Dear Diary,

In my heart I'm not a fighter. Never have been. I've had enough of the verbal sparring matches since I was a kid. Words thrown like grenades, tears and pain for days, not understanding how to win, or what there was to gain.

I liked the sound of silence and I liked being alone. Life was happier there. Even though I cried alone, it was better than crying in front of a finger in my face. Alone, I was free to be me: a dancer. I don't remember when I started, but I do remember dancing for Jesus, listening to a cassette tape, at an early age. My happy place. It stayed that way.

12.9
Baby Steps
Dear Diary,

The first time I was told I danced, was when I was 4-years-old.

A Christian band I don't remember the name of, was playing at my home church. Mom said everyone was standing up, and I was standing in the pew, dancing.

My little dance caught the attention of one of the band members, who tried to get me to come up on stage. Mom said I wouldn't go. I wonder how different my life would have gone, if I'd had the courage to go. To be brave. To dance for Jesus, up on stage. Someday I will. I pinky promise myself.

12.10
Dancing with Butterflies
Dear Diary,

The first time I remember dancing for someone, was for my dad.

A local church was having a talent show. My dad wanted to go, and sing a song with my brothers. I don't remember the name of it, but I do remember it was about Lazarus.

In an act of boldness and bravery, totally unlike me, I entered the talent show. I think I was 10. I don't remember getting the idea for it, or why I chose to. I just wanted to.

Dressed in a flowery skirt I had gotten at a thrift store, I danced to a song about butterflies and kisses.

I don't remember being nervous at all. I do remember twirling, and dreaming of the day I'd get to dance to the same song, wearing a white dress. My wedding dress, dancing on barefooted tippy-toes on daddy's shiny shoes. I'm glad I didn't know then, that dance, was as close as I would get.

12.11
David's Dance
Dear Diary,

The first time I snuck out of my parent's house was to dance in the rain for God. True story.

I was 14 when I slid my squeaking window up, praying it wouldn't wake my parents. My heart pounded. It would be worth it if I got caught and grounded.

Goosebumps, tickled my skin. Godbumps, as I prefer to call them, as they feel like a kiss from God to me. I always know He's with me when I feel them. At that moment, I wanted to feel like David did.

Little David from the Bible who cheated on multiple wives, danced for God, killed the big bad giant, played the harp, and yet God still chose him to be King. I can relate to most of that. Even had a harp though it got stolen by people I thought were my friends. What I loved the most, was imagining him dancing.

I imagined him dancing in the light of a blazing campfire. Singing, shouting, heart beating in his chest like a drum. Simply spending time with his Father, in a gleeful, playful, innocent way.

In my mind he never grew up. I wanted to feel that way for my Father too.

Slowly I removed the window screen and straddled the brick ledge. I turned, back to the lawn, and slid down behind the giant bush in front of my window. The bush was taller than me, I paused, hiding behind it. Barely believing I had just snuck out. I peeked around the edge of the green, and looked at a whole new world.

The moon shone above. Casting my front lawn in an almost magical spotlight. Streetlights glowed and flickered. Raindrops fell like diamonds from the sky. I stepped out, into the lamplight. My bare feet squished into the soft earth beneath the slippery grass. Godbumps rode my skin in waves. Something was happening. I stared up at the star-spangled sky, and smiled. I could feel God smiling down at me.

Mind and heart on God, no music, I began to dance in the rain. Just like David did.

12.13
Plastic Puppet People
Dear Diary,

I rarely found God in the southern Baptist mega church I grew up in. The wooden pews and stiff people, the plastic smiles and chairs, all too, hard. I imagined God a bit more, soft and free. Church shouldn't be clockwork, in my opinion, but this one was. 15 minutes of songs before the sermon, 12 after. I knew who, when, and where the people that were sitting, would stand up and raise their hands in praise. I could count on two of mine how many people there were. The pastor was one of the only good parts about that church, with a few good youth leaders over the years. He was a kind man, with a golden heart for God. I did learn a few things from him over the years. When he died, in my opinion, so did the church. I revisited it much later in life, and nearly walked out. But that's not a story that needs to be told yet.

This church felt more like a country club where the goers paid their dues by going to church, and felt entitled to the benefits of Jesus' death. There was little gratitude, little sincerity, and little real-life-ness. There was a high degree of formality, an air of expectation, and far too many copy and pasted, rinsed and repeated prayers. Most spoken in a monotone. I felt little feeling.

The Bible being such Good News why weren't the church goers, happier, my young mind wondered. Why weren't they excited? Why weren't they genuinely thanking God for His Son's incredibly painful death? Why weren't they dancing?

I danced. At 15 years old to a VHS concert tape of a popular Christian singer. My mom and brothers were at chess club. I had the house for a few hours. I'd put on the tape, turn up the volume louder than allowed, and dance. I got Godbumps there. That's where I felt God.

12.14

Prom Princess

Dear Diary,

Homeschoolers have prom, believe it or not. I went with a fellow long haired galfriend of mine named Jessa. Mom gave me $100 to get what I needed. I whined a little about the low amount, got over it, and went thrift shopping. $70 later, Jessa and I had matching Dark Angel outfits to attend the masquerade prom.

Black rose halos, black angel wings, and a black velvet dress covered in glitter, I felt beautiful. Jessa added the finishing touch with angel wings painted on our faces with eyeliner.

The ball began. She found some of her friends, and I found a one-night Prince Charming. A young dance teacher who swung me for hours that night. I danced, I sparkled, I twirled. I had a ball, and the time of my life.

12.15

Wedding Dance with Prince-Not-So-Charming

Dear Diary,

The wedding dance with my Prince Charming was sweet, but sour at the same time. We held each other, he twirled me. We did all the right things, but my heart wasn't all the way in it. It was too broken and bruised already.

12.16

Caged View

Dear Diary,

My fingers clasp the cage, eyes on the Jiu Jitsu fighters inside. My heart is pounding. Am I doing the right thing? Is this really going to work? I've been here 2 weeks already and I haven't done anything yet because I'm so scared. Feels like wasted time. These people are their own family. Rarely outside the ring do I see them. Tight knit, and strong, they seem, like their own army. The kind of people you want on your Zombie Apocalypse team. I want that.

As I watch, I listen. They use weird words like "backpack," "rear naked choke," "sweep," and "Ezekiel choke." Weird words I will one day understand.

I don't know if I can do this. Put myself back in the positions he did, relearn how to defend myself, and conquer all this fear. I don't want the last time I was in those positions, to be the time I failed by not defending myself. I want a second chance to fight, and to do it right.

"*I am scared,*" my heart said.

"Next up is sweeps from mount," Allen said.

"*This looks familiar,*" my mind said.

One guy straddled another laying on his back on the mat. Their arms move around like octopus tentacles. I don't know why. Top guy got his hands on the biceps of the one on the floor, pinning them to his sides like a cross. He puts his head on the guy's chest, and lays on him. Pinning him.

Flashback.

My Beast had done that. Though there was yelling, and, other things too, that happened. I could barely hear out of my left ear for 3 days. Right now, all I can hear is my blood roaring like a train in my brain.

"*I am not ok,*" my heart cried.

"Whoever is in mount, wait for their weight to shift," Allen said.

"*You will be ok,*" my mind said.

My knuckles are white, still gripping the cage. My eyes are blurring with tears. My heart is burning and breaking.

What am I doing here?! This isn't going to work! 2 weeks here and I'm already falling apart just from watching it! I can't do it! I am a ticking time bomb!

I want to walk away. Walk out of the gym. Go to therapy where my nightmare doesn't play out in front of my eyes. Where the only battle is with words and in my mind. I don't want to see it, I don't want to relive it. This was a terrible idea. I should have kept my bullshit out of my martial arts sanctuary.

The memories ran behind my eyes as life happened in front of me. Double vision at its worst.

"I am chicken shit," my heart said.

"Trap the leg, bridge, and sweep," Allen said.

"You are already further than you were," my mind said.

Fighting back the flood of tears, I forced myself to stay. In a blur of arm movements, the scene changed. The bottom guy, suddenly flipped, like a cartwheel with his knees, and was now on top! There was a way out.

"That was too easy!" my heart exclaimed.

"Make sure you take mount," Allen said.

"Where there is a will, there is a way," my mind smiled.

Fingers finally letting go of the cage, they clasped in a silent prayer.

"I feel, hope," my heart sighed in relief.

"Again," Allen said.

"I see a brave step taken," my mind smiled.

12.17

My Alcohol Veil

Dear Diary,

Life is a roller coaster. Yesterday was up, today I am down.

These memories aren't the only battle I fight: for years I have fought alcoholism. My addiction began the night I got raped. My sugar coat for my life's pain.

Last night I drank, today I paid.

A cold morning shower bandaided my hangover headache. A blast of nausea followed every pounding heartbeat. My stomach bubbled like an upside-down volcano. My thoughts had nowhere to go as my mind couldn't make up itself.

"Last time." How many times have I said that?

Tonight, I'll be going to kickboxing class hungover. The price I have/chose to pay. If I don't, alcohol wins. I'll try not to puke. My dirty little secret. It will be worth it in the end.

"Are you sure?" my heart asked.

"Last time," I said.

"Bullshit," said my mind.

...

I punched, I kicked, fighting back the waves of nausea.

My hangover lessened, when my eyes moved from my discomfort, to my goals. I wasn't fighting the hangover away. I was fighting to get one more push-up in before the bell rang.

Rock, or mountain moved? Depends on how close you look. Alcohol didn't beat me today.

12.18

No Thanks

Dear Diary,

"Someday I want you to look him in the eye and with the biggest smile on your face, thank him for every bruise, every name, everything he did that hurt you, because you know it made you into who you are now," Allen said.

"You have got to be kidding me! That Beast broke me! Thank him, ha! Thank him for handprints I couldn't wash off? For the blood? For the near broken bones? For all the 4 letter names he threw like grenades? It was hell! I should have given him a taste of his own medicine. I should have defended myself. I am not giving him a "Thank You." I have to deal with nightmares at night and flashbacks during the day while he is, whatever he is. Happy I hope." My words tumbled out of my mouth, building my defense around my still bleeding heart.

"Leslie, plants turn unbreathable carbon dioxide into breathable oxygen, right?" Allen asked.

"Yes."

"Think about what you can turn yourself into."

I wanted to argue, saying I am a broken, bedwetting body, still bleeding from the sting of internal wounds that won't yet heal. But, what good would that do? I am here to heal myself, with his help. To face the dragon, to fight my insecurities, to fight my PTSD, to paint over the ugly with the colors of happy. To take a life that nearly took my breath away, and write a happy ending. More than my defensive side wanted to argue, my optimistic side wanted him to be right.

12.19

Get up and Grind

Dear Diary,

Gym again, 5 days a week if my sore body can keep up with my determination. There may not be an entry every day. But there will be a step.

This is the part of the movie where you see the highlights of the daily grind. The soundtrack plays in the car ride from work. Fist pumping, chest pounding, yell-like-it's-your-last-breath music.

I'm still in the honeymoon phase. Happy to be home in martial arts again. Hungry for whatever is being served next. Hopeful for the happy ending I can't yet see.

I feel a little stronger these days. A little happier too.

12.20

Mind Over Me

Dear Diary,

"Don't let your body win over your mind," said Tyler, the coach of the circuit training class. Holding the dreaded plank, I prayed for strength. I despise plank position. More than burpees.

The timer seemed to move even slower as I dove into myself and pulled up every last drop of energy I had. Nothing mattered but not giving in. My clasped hands bounced like a pogo stick inches from the floor.

"Time!" he shouted. I collapsed. I did it!

Swells of pride flooded my body like a natural energy drink. I grinned great big. I could totally do that again. My body trembled as if to say, "Please no!"

There is a joke in here somewhere about holding and walking the plank, being a good thing, but I can't figure the words out.

12.21
3 Weeks
Dear Diary,

3 weeks ago, I was sitting in this same parking lot. A gleeful grin on my face as I imagined walking back into the arms of my beloved martial arts. Stars in my eyes at the thought of seeing my hero Allen again.

I gave up everything to be here. I spent a month mapping jobs and living opportunities, centering everything around the gym. I moved back home to Nashville from my beloved mountains. I got a job with a schedule that fit class times. Reduced from a 1-bedroom apartment to one bedroom. I sold or gave away everything else I had. Paying for a storage unit felt like paying for a gravesite to hold the remains of a life I no longer had. My money was better spent on a life-giving gym membership.

3 weeks down, strength is up, and in between I've learned sweat is tears in action.

"I am happier," my heart said.

"You need gas," the orange light said.

"You are doing well," my mind said.

12.23
Beginnings and Endings
Dear Diary,

Before I enter the ring, I want a one on one with Allen. I want him to put me back into my worst fear: a choke. I need to deal with it alone. Freak out, black out, cry if I want to. Let go safely and privately so as not to make a scene in class.

The really sad part, is that it wasn't my Beast that choked me first. It was, someone else.

I was trying to get away from him. Trying to leave his house, but he was doing everything in his power to stop me. He yelled, he blocked the doorway, he got physical.

TRIGGER WARNING

He came up behind me. His hands and arms slid around my neck. My life flashed before my eyes for the first time. It was in that moment, as I felt his strong arms squeeze my neck, as my breath became stuck in my lungs, I realized I could die.

I know this man would never kill me. But right there, right then, he could have. If he didn't let go, I couldn't get my breath back. Rock bottom is always further than I think.

He slammed me to the floor and drug me away from the door. He flung me to the floor, yelling at me for us to just talk.

"No!" I screamed. "I'm leaving, and this is why!"

Eventually I got out, and never looked back.

When my Beast's hands encircled my neck for the first time, it wasn't the defense against it, that flashed in my mind first. It was the memory of that man's hands.

"I've been here before," my mind said.

"Love doesn't do this!" my heart cried, every time.

I stayed silent, and cried.

Instead of enacting my training, I reacted in fear. I froze, mind lost and confused in the deja vu tailspin.

I'm scared I'm going to remember more as I go deeper. I'm scared to rinse and repeat my worst memories. But I don't know how else to do it right. I don't want to pay someone to hear me complain on a big comfy couch. I want to deal with it, right now.

"Maybe rinsing, will wash it clean," my heart hoped.

"Nightmares only exist in the dark," my mind said.

"I won't know until I do," I said.

"You will, Leslie. You're stronger than you think," my mind believed.

12.24

Pay it Backwards

Dear Diary,

A year before I met him, Prince Charming met and defeated his own dragon. One of those events that changes your life. He lost so much. Voices told him he couldn't, piles of evidence confirmed it. But he did. Through his own determination, he rebuilt and regained a miraculous amount back. He now shares his testimony to any and all open ears. His own happy ending he fought hard for.

As he told his story, I listened between the lines. I heard a story about a hardworking man. A man who beat impossible odds. I heard him laugh at the ways he fought. Somehow in the middle of the mess, he made fun. I saw pride in his eyes as he told me of his milestones. I saw the Lord light his eyes up. I heard him give credit to God. I felt my heart fall in love with him.

"If he can beat that, together, we can beat anything," my heart said.

"It was all because of God," he said.

"Actions speak louder than words," my mind said.

Karma is a bitch, right? I can be too. Here is that side of me. I have sometimes wondered if my Prince's own dragon, was a sort of, karmatic prepayment, for what he did to me. I cringed typing that.

Is it possible instead of paying for what he did to me, after the fact, was his own dragon, his prepayment price?

Do I want Beast to pay more? No, not really. At minimum I want him to understand what he did. What he did to me then, what it's doing to me now. I want him to care, that's all.

"What did I ever do to you?!" he asked during one of our last arguments. My only answer was a jaw drop. Either he was a better liar than I thought, or he was more blind than I knew.

I know my heart still bleeds from the wounds he gave me. Maybe he is still bleeding from his. The price he is paying, from his own dragon he is daily slaying, could be the same, as mine. Maybe him hurting me, was just him fighting back against the life that had hurt him too. Mask on, claws out, no one could hurt him, again.

"I will always love him," my heart said.

"I will always love you," my lips said at our last lawyer meeting.

"[Inaudible], too," he mumbled.

"He didn't love you," my mind said.

12.27

The Alcohol Story

Dear Diary,

Liquid courage for some, liquid bandaid for me. What was once a flavorful exploration, became a necessary intoxication. I wanted to forget what had happened. But I can't, so here it is.

TRIGGER WARNING

I was raped while I was sleeping by a male mentor. He was never prosecuted. Sometimes life is shit. I don't want to tell the rest of that story. Alcohol became my new best friend. The only way I knew how to escape my new reality, was to get black out drunk for the first time. So I did. For a long time.

"Your eyes aren't crying now," my heart noticed.

"It'll only take one more drink to get there, Leslie," my reflection said.

"Don't trust a friend you pay for," my mind chided.

I was 17 months sober when Prince Charming gave me the perfect excuse to drink again: celebration. If I went overboard, he would stop me. I had accountability now. Someone to hold me up when I needed them to.

"You won't let him stop you," my heart cheeked.

"Not too much honey," he said.

"You're kidding me right?" my mind said.

The day I moved in, my give a damn broke. I was drinking within 30 minutes of getting to my new home. I wanted that liquid courage. That ease of mind. The best part of me, I got at the beginning of drinking. I liked who I was when my walls were lowered. I felt free.

The damage my dam breaking did, lasted most of our relationship. I was a drunk Princess.

He came home, night after night, to find vomit, a project half finished, something cooking, and too many lights on in the house. That's all I remember, but I bet he can tell you a sadder story.

My nightmares, came to play, before I blacked out. All the memories I was too chicken shit to face, came pouring out with my tears. I was a mess.

I don't know why he stayed with me. I was drunk enough to drive anyone away.

I was drunk enough to defend myself. Sober I submitted, drunk I stood my wobbly ground and tried to stop him. He met me like a match, a match, he had to win. The sooner I submitted, the sooner he won, and walked away. At least I tried for a while. Until I learned I was safer submitting.

I cried my tears into a bottle. 2 years in, high up in the clouds of smoking weed, I found a happier escape. I wish I'd found weed sooner. My life would have been better, and rememberable.

12.28
The Suicide Story
Dear Diary,
TRIGGER WARNING

I decided one night, I wanted to end my life. I was beginning to see the shape-shifting shadow of my Prince turning into a Beast. Adding to the rape flashbacks lighting up my mind at that time, and loneliness in our bed at night, I decided. If this was a good or bad as life was going to get, I didn't want to live it anymore.

I drank a lot of alcohol, I drew a hot bubble bath, and my hand held a shiny thing. I wanted to die pretty.

As my tears popped the colorful bubbles, my mind began to relive my life. I saw little more than pain. I see no need in telling you the memories that played behind my crying eyes. Suffice to say when all you are looking for is the bad and sadness, that's all you will find. I saw brief flashes of my family crying at my funeral. Those made me sadder.

My suicidal pity party was crashed, when my Prince/Beast came home early from work. Instead of saving me, his actions, and words, added to my hurt. Behind the blur of tears and alcohol, I remember hearing and seeing ugly things. Things like his video camera light, and his voice, laughing.

It was then I began to see the castle my Beast was building around me. A prison of video evidence and my name on dotted lines. No obligations or responsibilities holding him close to me. I began to wonder if he was planning his escape. At our unhappy ending, all debts and titles were in my name, and he had nothing to lose. He was free, and I was up shit's creek, without a paddle. I was financially drowning.

Somehow, in the still clear water of the bathtub that night, I survived. I don't remember how the night ended. I do remember the doubt that attached itself to me, like an unfriendly shadow. All the alcohol I drank over the next years, couldn't hide the mistake I knew I had made.

Some Beasts turn into Princes. Some Princes turn into Beasts. Sometimes they are both.

12.31

Dance Hands

Dear Diary,

Maybe it's crazy to think, much less believe, that manifest destiny, can create, what I want to see.

The first thing I want to see, when I close my mortal eyes, is Jesus' nail scarred Hand, asking me to dance. I'll take His hand, I'll float onto His feet, stepping onto His toes, and over the nail holes, off to Our Father's House we will go.

JANUARY'S F8TH

January 2nd
Closed Door
Dear Diary,
    I miss love and hugs. I just watched Allen hug his woman, her name is Prydacted. It was a sweet hug, during the middle of class. The kind that says, "I still see you."
    I smiled.
    "You'll never have that again," my heart said.
    "Better to have loved and lost than never to have loved at all," Alfred Lord Tennyson.
    "Arguable," my mind said.
    Tears sprung to my eyes as I watched. Heartbreak healing was happening. I miss it, love. As hard as the love I had for my Prince was, I still loved loving him. Having him meant everything meant something. Even buying toilet paper: I found his favorite. I smiled.
    I don't believe I'll have a fairytale, again. I believe I have to give up a love story with a man, to get a dream with myself. I can't be up on stage, showing how God fills all holes, when I have a man to come home to fill mine. It has to be just Him. It's a bit lonely at times, but I believe it's better this way.
    I felt a chapter close in my heart. A soft thud, nothing forced or unwanted. Like a book closing. I still want love, but unless it's that football player who wrote John 3:16 on his cheeks, Tim Tebow, I'm not interested. That man loves the Lord.
    As the chapter closed, I felt like I was riding a surfboard down a river. A river flowing down a hallway flanked by life-shaped doors. As this heart-shaped door closed, my current became a little stronger.
    One less hole to peer through, to cry into, to allow the outside in.
    I feel a little more whole.
    This feels like a good thing.

1.3

Let's Play a Game

Dear Diary,

"The dragon will always be there," Allen said. "His job is to make you afraid. If you beat him do you really think he won't get up and try again? He will always try. He wants to destroy you. He doesn't want you to live free."

His words echoed in my mind as my eyes watched the Jiu Jitsu fighters. I had foolishly thought once I'd beaten the dragon at the end of this journey he wouldn't respawn. But many people who beat the game, go back and beat it again, better. It's never game over. Does that mean I'll always be living with and fighting against these flashbacks? That's not the end game I was hoping for. I don't know where to go from here.

1.5

I Always Lost the Game

Dear Diary,

It was my fault, he always said. The same hands doing the damage, pointed a finger into my wound, and said I pulled the trigger.

"If you wouldn't argue with me so much this wouldn't happen."

"If you would get your head out of your ass, you might be able to hear what I'm trying to tell you."

"I'm just trying to get your attention; my words aren't working anymore."

"I wasn't like this before I met you. I hate the man you have turned me into."

"I didn't hit you, the *object* did."

"I am sorry, but you…"

"If you weren't such a *bad name* first, I wouldn't have to be this way."

I could go on and on, but I don't want to continue down that way.

What I heard and learned from his words are these points:

It was all my fault. He just wanted me to agree with him, always.

The "c" word made my blood boil. I felt close to anger, which scared me.

Telling him what he did that hurt me, did nothing but up his ammunition. I told him I didn't like the "c" word, it became his favorite.

There are countless ways to submit, though I thought I was being smart. Smart by lying and telling him I agreed. Smart by never again telling him what hurt me. Smart by telling him whatever it seemed like he wanted to hear. Smart by doing whatever it took to keep him from becoming violent. It didn't work. He found a way, almost every weekend.

One time, I heard more emotion in his "I'm sorry," than ever. I almost believed he meant it. I still wonder if he did.

It was a time when, in the way he hurt me, he had to help me. I was wounded and could not physically fix my body. I either needed a hospital or him. He had a choice, and he made the right one. I was selfishly relieved. For the first time ever, he couldn't walk away from the damage he had done. Well, he could have, but he knew I needed help, and he chose to help me.

As I lay on my stomach on the towels on our bed, my tears flowed and his words poked his finger into my back. I heard a balancing act. Emotion flowed between the blame, and what sounded like a genuine apology. I'd never heard that from him before.

I lay there, longer than a 5-minute fix. I listened, and cried into the towels both from emotional and physical pain.

"See? He loves me," my heart sighed in relief.

"I love you but sometimes you make me hate you," he said.

"Jesus never said that," my mind shouted.

It was on this day, my mind formed the worst words it had ever put together.

"Maybe now he has hurt me bad enough, he will feel bad, and stop." Yes, yes, I did think that. And no, no, he didn't stop. Red flags often come dressed in different colors.

The hardest part, was knowing he was right when he said it wasn't him who hit me. It was objects, furniture, the floor where I landed.

He was right. How could I argue against fact?

You can't win against someone who always changes the game. That's why they say, the only way to win, or survive, in this case, is to get away.

1.7
Paint by Words
Dear Diary,

For every bruise and blood drop, I had pretty words to paint over them. Life is what you make of it right? Build a fairytale, by looking at the happy, that's not a lie, right? It's seeing the best of life by choosing a better perspective, Einstein taught me so.

Sugar is only supposed to coat, I was creating an invisibility cloak. Refusing to believe what was really happening, because I didn't want to believe it was happening to me.

I didn't want to believe I chose the wrong Prince Charming. I didn't want to believe I had become a Damsel in Distress, instead of a Princess. I didn't want to believe love hurt that much. I had poured so much sugar over my life, I had caramelized a lie.

1.10
Redirect
Dear Diary,

"The closer you are to danger the further you are from harm," Allen said. He pointed to his chest, then pointed to the tip of the sword he was holding.

What the heck does that mean?

The John 3:16 football player got engaged yesterday, to Ms. Universe. Bummer.

1.11
Do You Believe in Fairytales?

Dear Diary,

 Believing the best in people has cost me more than anything. Believing that people will choose good, do good, be good to one another, while the actions in front of my eyes, and the evidence on my body, speak otherwise. I'll never stop believing.

 I've seen enough bad to ruin my belief. From the monsters I imagined on the outside of my homeschooled walls, to the men leading life with iron fingers, to realizing the worst monsters are within people, I've seen enough, to ruin me.

 But I still believe in happy endings, like the Bible. At its simplest, the Bible is a story of a God who made some kids, us. He calls us Princes and Princesses. We ran away from Him and home. So He made a special Son/King to pay for, with His life, the golden ticket home to heaven through redemption. Then, at the end of time, that same special Son/King is coming back on a white horse to bring us home.

 Life is a fairytale.

 I'll never stop believing.

1.14

The First Step

Dear Diary,

 "When are we going to do it?" I asked, nodding my head towards the ring.

 "I don't know yet," Allen said.

 Adrenaline, bravery, and impulsiveness surging, my quivering voice asked, "How about now?"

 His eyes flickered as they met mine. He knew something.

 "How about I one up you?" he challenged.

 Nervous but excited, my heart sped up.

 "Stand up."

 Without hesitation I stood.

 What I thought was going to be his hands around my neck, turned out to be one small step.

He corrected my stance and explained distancing between me and my opponent.

"Why are we starting here?"

"Steps," he said. "If you go head on into something it will hit you back. Trust me."

"I do."

He showed me a defense called the Double Forward Block: hands on my forehead, elbows together.

It was then that I realized this was going to be a much slower process than I'd wanted. I'm a go-getter that doesn't know when to quit. I've been here a month and already want to face my dragon without setting my foundation, as he was teaching me to do. Not in the ring, but on the floor in front of it. Steps.

He used a blue pool noodle to swing. He swung, and in the blur I saw the memory. I saw the paddle of childhood being swung, not Allen swinging the noodle, and I crumbled a bit inside. On the outside I stood there and took it, as I always had, and had to.

I took a breath, stood a little taller, and readied. He swung. I didn't even blink. Just stood there and took it, again. I used to go to a dark place in my mind, before the paddle hit my behind, refusing to let any form of emotion show on the outside. I didn't like that place, but it was better than crying.

"Defend yourself Leslie, I just showed you how," Allen said.

My mind pulled my head and heart back down to earth. I wasn't there anymore. I didn't need to be. I was here, growing. Guilt pricked at my heart, I shoved it away. I stanced and readied.

He swung, I blocked, again, again, and again.

He swung again, thinking I was smart, I grabbed it.

He bopped me on the head with his other noodle.

"Why did you do that?!" I asked, irritated.

"When you react with emotion, you open yourself up. It leaves you vulnerable. Defend yourself, Leslie."

We went a few more rounds, then my questions began.

As we talked, I learned I hide behind questions. Always asking why, when I should be watching how, and just doing what he said. Allen said I kept pushing my questions, and my version of how, instead of letting him lead me, step by step. I wanted to face my fear dead-head on. He wanted to help me prevent it from happening again. He told me today was a test on how I dealt with adversity. I questioned it. Hiding behind wide eyes and limp hands. I just wanted to know why, and to do my path my way. I didn't want to do the work, or believe I'd have to do it step by step, just like everybody else.

Allen taught me today to do what I came here to do and trust him. Let him show me the steps to take to walk the path to my happy ending.

My problem will be getting outside of my head and heart and just doing what needs to be done.

Fueled by bravery and birthing momentum, I pushed myself into a boxing techniques class, later that day.

A class where Allen incorporated what he had taught me just a few hours earlier. I half suspected he would. That's who he is. You never know what he is up to. I knew what he was doing: helping me build momentum by implementing our one on one into class to further solidify my foundation. He truly is my hero.

I trained with my partner, reveling in the healing energy hanging in the room. This rinse and repeat felt like renewal.

After class I smiled one of the biggest smiles of my life and said,

"Thank you. I know what you did."

A knowing smile split his face as he said, "Now you're learning."

"I realize now I asked you for my first step today. I'd been waiting for you to lead, but I did it."

Smile deepening on his face, he said, "I know. You needed to. You needed to get to a point of being frustrated enough to ask when we were going to get this going. It's part of the steps."

Have you ever felt like you were exactly where you were supposed to be, at the exact right time? I'm there. Today. Right now. Typing my story on the couch next to the door as Allen sits

15 feet away on his work computer. I'm meant to be here. It feels like a footprint I fit into.

1.23

The Great Physician

Dear Diary,

I woke up, and decided I'm going to enter the ring tonight, it's time. I want to do this. I'm not "ready" but I realized I never will be. I just have to do it.

My devotional this morning talked about those moments we are "here," in a place that used to be "there." I'm taking that as God's way of confirming it is time.

It's time for this. Allen said he'd choose when I am ready for the hard stuff, but I'm choosing this one. In a couple hours I'm going to walk into that gym and ask him to choke me before my first class.

It's time to look my dragon in the eye.

...

Allen isn't here. I'm running out of time so I just walked into the ring by myself. I'll figure out something to do. I'm sitting in the middle of it. Prydacted is here so I'm a bit bashful to cry if I need to.

"I don't know what to do," my heart said.

Silence, in the gym.

"Do something," my mind said.

Tonight, I'm facing my dragon, in front of other people without having done it with Allen first. Can I really do this?

"I can't do this," my heart said.

Silence, in the gym.

"Yes, you can Leslie," my mind believed.

...

My music began to play as I lay in the middle of the ring, phone to my left, laptop protectively on my lap. Fluorescent lights overhead, like a surgeon's table. Legs crossed at my ankles; arms clasped over my chest. I used to lie like this during my self-therapy sessions where, in my mind I tried to fight my memories by rinsing and repeating them until I washed the bad feelings clean. It didn't work. Though I tried for years.

As the music played, God firmly but gently told me to relax, uncross my legs, move the laptop to the floor, spread my arms, and let Him operate. I fought Him. Tears beginning to fall, I held onto myself, arms wrapped tightly around my chest.

"I don't want to look like a fool," I argued.

"Sometimes you have to. Jesus looked a fool to those who didn't know what He was doing," God said. I relented. I moved the laptop.

"Uncross your ankles."

"That will look wrong God."

"Not when they read your book and know what you were doing." He was right, as always.

"Spread your arms."

"But God I already look nuts! Tears and sobs in a gym in front of who knows who else has shown up, is not normal, it's crazy. I don't want to cause a scene or upset Allen or Prydacted with my behavior," I argued.

"I'll take care of it. Like I'm taking care of you now."

Like a child who didn't want to eat her vegetables, I moved my arms above my head. Open. Vulnerable.

The lights above flashed like lightning, back to my past.

I had been here before. Trapped beneath his hands and knees.

I couldn't move then. I felt and heard it all over again. I felt God's Power swoop in. It was time for heart surgery.

My Beast's face came into view above me. He was smiling, like he sometimes did. My blood began to boil, as close to anger as I go. I saw God's Hand wipe it away.

Then He asked the one question I am most afraid of, "What are you truly afraid of Leslie?"

My heart spoke the truth before my mind could find the answer, "Love hurts."

I watched in my mind's 3rd eye as my life played its lowlight reel.

I saw myself, the tears through the years. I saw how I had let my bedwetting dehumanize me. Every morning, waking up unclean, and unfit to join humanity. Every morning, waking up, afraid.

I saw the ends of pointing fingers, heard the yelling in my ears. Telling me my feelings were wrong, telling me I was guilty for mine and the actions of others.

I saw my Prince, who turned into my Beast. Who went from loving to hating me. From telling me he thought I was beautiful, to blaming me. From massages to manhandling me. Though sometimes his eyes would go pale, I could still see my Prince within my Beast.

I saw my sweet mom, who loves unconditionally. Who hugs me when I cry, who always knows what to say, whose actions live the love of God. She is the best mom, everyone who meets her says the same. She loves me, and I want to be just like her someday.

I saw my sweet Jesus, smiling and saying He loves me too.

Ripples of sorrow rode my body like a bull. I sobbed on the floor of the ring. As quietly as I could, I let go.

"Why are you reliving pain Leslie? You're not living there anymore."

Before the tears had emptied, I felt a door close. God said it was enough.

I saw white smoke, in my 3rd eye, like that from dry ice, pour from a spot a few feet below the black ceiling. It flowed like a waterfall over my body, filling me with what I can only describe as vigor. A surge of pure energy, it was in my bones and blood, seeping out through my pores. The next image took over my mind as my arms spread wide: I was jumping out of a plane, by myself this time. I was taking flight. I was diving and soaring through the sky as the white smoke took the shape of clouds. I was flying free. Finally, free. I wanted to stay there forever.

"Let's do this."

"What do you mean?" Allen asked

"I want you to choke me before class, after I wash off these mascara tears."

"I have to work first," he said, his hands encircling the gym.

"Ok, I just wanted you to do it before I'm in front of everyone."

"Don't worry about them, they will be doing their own thing and not paying any attention. Trust me."

"I do."

1.24

Game On

Dear Diary,

I feel like a mighty warrior! Let me tell you the fairytale I lived yesterday!

I was sitting on the couch next to the ring, finishing up typing the story. The Jiu Jitsu fighters began to show and warm up.

I shut the laptop down, and went to the bathroom. I knelt and prayed there. I'm still a bit shy to pray in public. I walked out, and walked towards the ring. Allen watched me.

My heart was pounding, my hands, cold and clammy. My bare feet walked the black steps up to the ring. Cold steel against my cold hands. I pushed the door open as a wave hit me.

Fear hit me first, backed by bravery. Determination followed closely behind, holding hands with excitement.

"I'm so nervous!" my heart squealed.

"No one in there is going to hurt you," Allen had said. *"You're doing it!"* my mind cheered.

We bowed in, paired off, and began. I was paired with a young and feisty blonde girl named Miranda.

Allen said we were learning 4 ground defenses. He picked Miranda as his partner to demonstrate.

The moves came easily, my fear stayed fairly quiet, and my excitement grew. My memory of the first 2 defenses has a blank space over it.

"Now we are going to work on the defense against an Ezekiel choke." My heart sunk, my mind reeled, and I panicked.

"No! No! No! I can't do this yet! I'm not ready! This is too much! I'm too scared!" my heart screamed.

"Let's get into position," Allen said.

"You'll never be ready, Leslie, you just have to do it. Don't let fear win," my mind reasoned.

Allen eyed me. Our eyes met, for a moment I let my wall down so he could see how freaked out I was. I wanted to cry, to puke, to run, for him to do any move but the choke. My feelings didn't change his mind or his plan.

As we broke off into our pairs, myself with Miranda, I asked her to hold off. I caught Allen's eye and asked him to do the first choke. He nodded.

He knelt over my hips, pinning me. Time seemed to slow as I watched his hands lower towards me. Like handcuffs, they encircled my neck. I was trapped.

Suddenly I wasn't there. I was in our house, on our bed, on the hallway floor, standing in the living room. Terror struck my heart like lightning. Through the flash I saw Allen's face still above me. His eyes beamed as if to say, "Come back Leslie." I blinked, and the memories faded away.

As I "swept" him, my hands trembled, and a sob burst from my lips.

Allen saw it, and stayed still, letting me let it out.

It was over. I had done it.

"Thank God that's over!" my heart sighed.

"Good job," Allen said.

"See? You did it Leslie," my mind smiled.

Rinse and repeat with Miranda. Fun began to replace fear with each drill we did.

"Last up is the snow angel defense," Allen said. He pinned Miranda's arms above her head on the floor. Oh shit.

Another one of my worst fears. Why was he doing another one?! I swallowed back fear and tears.

"Not again! This is too much! I can't handle this!" my heart cried.

"Swipe your arms down, pull your knees up, and grip them. They can't hit you if you hold them close to you," Allen said. "The closer you are to danger, the further you are from harm."

"You just did it Leslie. Do it again," my mind reassured.

I pulled myself out of my head and into Allen's instructions. Again, I asked him to do the first one for my own safety net.

As my arms went up, my heart flashed in a newfound feeling. I really disliked the vulnerability of having my arms above my head. It nearly made me mad. Felt like a cheap shot. A shot Beast had made many times. I felt indignation rising. I shoved it aside. It would do me no good here.

I looked up. My Beast's face smiled down at me from my memories. I blinked back down to earth where it was Allen's face in my reality. Step by step I made my moves. Relief flooded my body as I became free again. I did it. It was over.

"You need to stop underestimating yourself Leslie," my mind said.

"That was terrifying and satisfying," my heart said.

"I did it," I said.

"Lastly we are going to go a couple rounds of free-rolling," Allen said. "This is optional. We have a lot of new people here so if you aren't comfortable with it you don't have to do it."

Miranda and I began. I had no idea what to do other than keep her from pinning me down. It felt like somersaulting. My adrenaline spiked, and fear stayed away. I began to laugh. It was fun.

3 minutes flew by in a blur of absolute glee.

From lying on the floor with her on top of me, I swept and mounted Miranda.

"Nice! That was your first sweep!" she said. I grinned.

"I did it!" my heart exclaimed.

"Switch partners," Allen said.

"I told you so," my mind smiled.

As we bowed out, I wanted more. Said a quick prayer and thanked God for surpassing my dreams with reality.

I thanked Allen, and proudly told him about my first sweep. He smiled like he knew something I didn't.

"Everything comes in due time, when you are ready. What you have to understand is that life will always come at you from different angles. You just have to tweak what you know to fit the situations as they come, in life and Jiu Jitsu."

I hugged Miranda, telling her anytime she saw me writing and wanted to "roll" I would. She smiled at me.

Not wanting to create a scene, I waited until the gym was empty, to freak out a bit on Allen.

"Dude, why did you do the choke and the pin in my first class?! I wasn't ready for that!"

"Because that's what you came here for," he said.

1.25

Recap

Dear Diary,

"Got a few bumps and bruises yesterday, but I did learn I could push through it and just fight," I told Allen. "I've never fought like that before, not even with my brothers."

"See? I told you you'd be ok. I like to keep things short enough to where no one gets truly hurt. Most Jiu Jitsu classes practice for 2 hours and all you walk away with is injury and knowing someone tougher than you can beat your ass."

"That's that's what I'm afraid of. I don't want to go full force because I'm worried about hurting someone."

"It's not hurting someone, it's defending yourself. When I kick someone, I have a 50/50 chance of hurting myself. Why?"

"You could do it wrong."

"Exactly. I know I'm taking that risk. It's not hurt, it's karma. No one in that ring is out to hurt you, they are out to defend themselves. Hurting means there is ill-intent from the offender. Defense is self-preservation from the defender."

Like pieces of a jigsaw puzzle, his words fell into place in my mind. His reasons are right. I'm just full of excuses.

1.26

A Piece of Game

Dear Diary,

For the last 2 days I have replayed that night in the ring easily 1000 times. One of the proudest moments of my life. My first giant leap into this new life of mine. Rinsing and repeating the memory made me realize I had a blank space over several seconds of it. Allen will know why tonight.

"Allen, 2 days ago in the ring, I blacked out. I remember seeing you walking halfway across the ring towards me to do the choke. The next thing I remember is you on top of me. How you got there is gone. Is that, ok? I've never blacked out like that before."

"Sometimes the mind does that to protect us from things it doesn't want to remember. But it is ok. You'll get through this."

"I do have memories of him smiling, at inopportune times. I don't want to believe they are real, but not so deep down I know they are. I even remember him grinning when I told him I wouldn't call the cops on him. Why would he do something like that?"

"It's all fun and games when you take the danger away," Allen said.

"A game?!" I shrieked. "To what end?!"

Allen chuckled, "To win. What else?"

Eyes brimming with tears, I stared at him.

"So, what was I?"

"Something to make him feel better about himself. A pawn, opponent, not his Queen. That's why he smiled. You were a stepping stone."

"No," my heart said.

"Yes," Allen said.

"You already know," my mind said.

Truth really hurts sometimes.

1.28

Love and Loss

Dear Diary,

You'd think after 3 and a half years of his cons, I would have learned better, by now. You'd think I'd be able to recognize the red flags dressed in different colors. But I didn't. Because hiding the red flags, was the glitter I poured over life in the name of Fairytale. I blinded myself.

"Here, let me see your phone," his words spoke his last con. The one I should have learned to see by now. It was a year after our unhappy ending, and we were finally getting around to splitting up the last of our assets. He refused to give me the lawyer's address, and insisted on a personal meeting prior.

The red flags were flying in front of my still love blind eyes. Personal meeting at a dead end, I followed him to the parking lot of the restaurant, still asking for the lawyer's address. "Here, let me see your phone," he said. In one of the stupidest moments of my life, I trusted him, again. With no good reason for doing so.

I wish I could go back to that moment. Tell naive Leslie to stop believing what isn't there. Tell her she knows he is in it for himself, that's what con artists do. They lie, cheat, and steal. I'd tell her do not give him your phone that is still in his name. It would be one of the costliest mistakes of her gullible life.

It was. Still believing the best in him, despite all the bullshit, I gave him my phone, and got the sickest smirk of a smile in return. As well as the spotlight of the camera his lover was recording on in the background. I had been set up. Into his back pocket my phone went, his vibes and his eyes changed, and in a tone slick as ice, he said, "This is mine. I've already called the phone company and the police; you can't do anything."

I could tell you the details of the rest of the story, but I see no need. Suffice to say I had my first major panic attack. I reached for the phone, and was later served Order of Protection papers by the police, which I foolishly said yes to in court. I thought it would finally keep him away, and myself safe. I didn't read the fine print, and by the time I did, I had to hire a lawyer to get it rescinded. The life cost was too high.

I lost so much that day, out of my own sheer stupidity. I lost my contacts because I hadn't backed them up. I lost the rest of the pictures of his violence I had yet to print. I lost my privacy, because I didn't have a password on my phone, which he went through. I know he did, because he responded to it, in his own way.

For the next 6 months, I woke up retching. The thought of him and his lover going through my phone, my life, my privacy, felt like a form of rape. I vomited so violently, my face began to hemorrhage. I still have scars from the blood vessels that couldn't heal. My blood was boiling.

Stupid stupid stupid Leslie. Looking back, all of my mistakes, all of the prices I have paid, I could have avoided, if I had led with my head, and not my heart. Not with my dreamer head in the clouds, but the one that sees reality. Sees the truth, not just what I want to believe.

1.29
Picture to Tear
Dear Diary,

In the corner of the gym, I put my headphones in, and laid the pictures of evidence on the floor around one of the hanging body bags.

As the pictures were laid, the memories came. I knew they would. I let my mind wander back to the past. Not reliving the memories, not caught off guard by the flashbacks, but simply seeing the scenes play.

The feelings in my chest started to swirl. Too many to name.

I tried to cultivate the "bad" feelings. Adding them to a volcano I wanted to erupt on the bag. It was hard, because I don't let myself get mad. I've seen what it does to people. It's safer to simmer in sadness. But sadness doesn't go anywhere. Nor does it do anything but simmer and hurt. I wanted to get mad at him for all he did to me, then I wanted to beat it out of my system.

I stood over the pictures I have. Staring, remembering, feeling, and bleeding on the inside.

"Which one do I hit?" my heart asked.

"What did I ever do to you?" he had asked during a final argument.

"This," my mind answered.

TRIGGER WARNING

My fingers found a picture from when his strong arms wrenched the wooden porch railing off its post, and threw it at me. Oh wait, he didn't hit me, the railing did. His shouting voice told me so after I cried out in pain from a near broken foot and arm I had raised to block it from hitting my face.

I taped the picture to the bag. I stared. I felt, both in my heart and on my body where the bruises used to be. It was one of those times I had hoped my bruises were big enough for him to see he needed to stop.

"Love doesn't do this," my heart ached.

"Don't fucking stand in my way you ignorant bitch!" he blamed.

"Love does this," my mind drew a heart around the gym.

Tears began to flow; I began to punch.

I wanted an eruption. But as per my usual, it came in waves. I don't remember for how long I punched. My goal was to punch until it tore in half. I was only crinkling the paper and my painter's tape wasn't sticking.

After a few rounds, I had an idea. The floor body bag.

I sat, straddling the bag's body, picture taped to the head. It was then the bad feelings started to flow.

How many times had he put me in this position? Pinned, trapped, using his strong body to stop me from moving. How many times could I not breathe? How many times did the pain take my breath away? How many tears fell as I cleaned up blood or broken things? Too many. 3 years too many.

My heart was now bleeding, from bodily wounds long ago healed.

I punched. SMACK. More of an impact sound than on the upright bag. I was stronger here.

I kept punching. I remembered a few ground and pound techniques from my Ernie Reyes days. I kept punching the picture. Purging out my bleeding heart.

The picture began to tear.

I punched. I imagined myself back in time. Back in those times. I imagined punching him away from me. Taking his breath away as he had mine, so many times. I imagined the look on his face. I imagined the happy ending I could have lived, had I done what I needed to do. I punched and pounded that picture. Giving it everything I wish I had given my past and myself. I jumped up, airborne, slammed the hardest hammer fist I could, and let out a kihap as my fists made impact.

The picture tore in half.

I gasped.

"You did it," my heart said.

Silence, save for my heart beating a little stronger now. *"I did it,"* my mind said.

I stared, I reveled, I savored, I breathed.

When I used to cry myself to sleep at night, I would try to cry until my tears ran out. I thought if I could cry until my body dried up, I'd be fine. Took me a year to figure out bodies don't dry up like that. Sometimes, you just have to draw the line, to tear the line.

I still have the picture. I'll burn it one day...

1.30

Direction

Dear Diary,

"I still want you to put me in a standing choke, the one from our Ernie Reyes days. The one my Beast put me in too. I want a second chance to defend myself, the way I should have all those times.

"It will happen in due time. Just trust me, "Allen said.

I growled.

"That sounds like frustration."

"Why is that a bad thing?"

"I didn't say it was a bad thing, did I? You have to remember that just because you aren't going forwards doesn't mean you are going backwards."

"There's just so much I want to do."

"It will come in time. When you decide you have a purpose, the universe will challenge you in every way. You have to keep the focus and prove you really want it."

It was challenging me. I went ice skating Saturday night, fallen, and possibly gotten a concussion. Jiu Jitsu class the next day seemed too dangerous. I spent what was supposed to be my second day fighting in the ring, sleeping in the dark, trying to get the world back to normal.

Even now, as I'm sitting at the gym writing this story, I'm being challenged. A photoshoot is happening. The flash of the camera light is hurting my head. I feel the pricks of a seizure starting. I am not ok right now.

As always, God took care of me. As I turned my back to the flashing light, God put a little miracle, in front of my face. A beautiful little 1-year old girl was toddling over to me. She smiled at me beneath her dark curls and long lashes. My heart warmed. Babies are magic for me. Pure and playful magic. I set my laptop down and began to play with her, after getting a nodding glance from her mom.

She shrieked as I chased her around the steel machines. She laughed as I tickled her belly button. She giggled as I tossed her in the air. She wrapped her little arms around my neck as I caught her on the way down. She punched the bag after I showed her how.

My heart danced within my chest. I smiled, I laughed, I wanted to cry. The seizure had been swept away, by a beautiful little girl, who wanted to play.

God always knows what to do.

My head isn't ok. I am still woozy and discombobulated. But I am ok. I will get through this.

FEBRUARY'S LIFE L9

Trigger Warning
February 1st
When Love Became a Choice
Dear Diary,
People have often asked me if I ever hit rock bottom. I did. Or rather, the murky green carpet. I fell out of love with him one day. Love became a choice, not a feeling.

I'm about to tell you an R-rated story. The choice to read, or skip, is up to you. Reader discretion is advised for violence, disturbing images, verbal assault, and general ugliness.

We were arguing, about what I don't remember. I wish I did. Words are often the breadcrumbs, to the burnt gingerbread house.

I was standing at the end of the hallway, in the living room. Behind me was 20 feet of hallway, 4 doors lining the walls, and our bedroom at the end.

The argument was normal. He had yet to become violent, but he was on his way. He was heated, nearly shouting.

Suddenly there was a blast, but it wasn't the back door whipping open in the mountain wind as it occasionally did. It was me, flying through the air.

My Beast's hands, had shoved me. I was airborne, flying over the murky green carpet. Past the doors, landing on the floor in front of our bedroom at the far end of the hallway.

I hit, and collapsed, paralyzed. My breath was knocked out of me, for the second time in my life. My mind flashed back to when I was 10 years old and had fallen off my swing set slide. I thought I was dying then, until my breath came back. I never told my mom. I didn't want her to worry. My mind now knew it was going to burn and hurt for a few minutes, but I was going to be ok.

I tried to gasp, but couldn't. I tried to move, but couldn't. It was like my nerves were roadblocked before direction could reach my fingertips. My breath was stuck. My lungs stung. It felt like a giant was sitting on my chest. It hurt horribly.

It was about to get worse.

As I lay, paralyzed, barely able to gasp for air, he sauntered over. He was smiling again. His eyes had changed color again.

Shit.

All this I saw through the tears somehow seeping from my eyes.

He knelt, next to my panicking and paralyzed self. He began to laugh. I began to pray.

"You fucking little pussy!" he said.

"No!" my heart cried.

"You cunt!" he said.

"I can't stand that word!" my heart screamed.

"One little fall and you've burst into tears like a weak-ass little whiny girl."

"Stop stop stop!" my heart cried.

I still couldn't breathe or speak.

"Face the truth, Leslie," my mind steered. *"Don't hide in your dreams."*

"You're such a cunt! A fucking little bitch-ass pussy! You're so weak! Look at you, lying on the floor crying like a blubbering baby. Fucking cunt. Stop pretending like you're dying. Get your fat ass up."

So many words, while I struggled for just one breath.

"Why would love do this?!" my heart begged to know.

"I hate you!" he said.

"It doesn't," my mind spoke in stone.

It wasn't over.

Rock bottom came next.

It wasn't the first time, it wasn't the last, but it was the worst time. He hacked, and spat, a lugi in my face.

It was too much.

I felt something change in my chest. I don't know if something broke or a subconscious wall was built, but it hurt. My heart fell. Fell out of love. I felt it. I felt the butterflies burn to death by his words.

"*I don't want to feel like this anymore,*" my heart cried.

"*I don't want him,*" my heart continued.

"*I don't want this,*" my heart admitted.

His venomous words kept falling, but I don't want to write those down.

"*Love is a choice,*" my mind said.

"*God, I need You right now!*" my heart cried.

"*I love you, I'm here,*" He spoke.

Rock bottom, took another step down.

Beast stood, his steel-toed boots began to kick me, as his voice continued to laugh and taunt.

The most painful thought I've ever had, entered my mind then: I could love and forgive him more than he could hurt me. It's bullshit but it's true. Love had become my choice.

I wish I could go back to that moment, to that woman on the floor in a puddle of heartbreak.

I'd tell her while her intentions were pure, they were heading in the wrong direction.

I'd tell her, loving him, could be done from afar.

I'd tell her, dying at Beast's hands, would not make her a martyr for love. I'd tell her to love him less, and herself more.

I'd tell her while it is true by faith all things are possible, not all things are supposed to happen. There is more than one fairytale ending to choose from.

I'd tell her to choose herself, it's not selfish. Submissive wife didn't mean becoming his puppet.

I'd tell her she mattered too, but she didn't matter much to him.

I'd tell her by staying, she was allowing him to hurt her.

I'd tell her the cold hard truth: he wanted to hurt her.

It's why he laughed. It's why he smiled. He liked it.

It's bullshit, but it's true.

2.3

Lying to Mom

Dear Diary,

I loved my weekly talks with my mom. Books, movies, things we were cooking or doing, we would talk for hours. She never knew I was lying to her. She'd ask how things were going, I'd say they were going well. I could have, should have, but wouldn't tell her the truth.

Hiding, and lying, pretending everything was fine, to her, the most loving heart I've ever met, was one of the hardest things I've ever done.

Countless nights, as he simmered playing video games and I cried in our bedroom I wanted to call my mom.

I wanted to call and tell her everything. I wanted to tell her I'd made a mistake. Either about him or about what love was. Love wasn't supposed to hurt this way, was it? I wanted her to somehow make it ok. Even if all she did was listen and tell me I needed to leave, I wish I could have listened. I wish I would have told her.

I couldn't break her heart, so I didn't.

As much as my memories hurt me by living them, I believe it would, in a way, hurt her worse to know them.

2.4

Abracadabra

Dear Diary,

After Jiu Jitsu class today, I got to train with a guy named Shelby who has long flowing hair that makes even me jealous, and a guy named Cody.

They taught me submissions, positions, and how to change my game based on body types.

We drilled and rolled for a while, when all of a sudden, Shelby said one of my magic words.

"Be intense this round," Shelby said.

I've always been described as intense and passionate. Problem is, I've had nowhere to put it. I do know what it feels like.

Arms and legs free of mental shackles, I moved with a fluidity I didn't know my bones could maneuver. Led by touch, eyesight secondary, I moved until something felt right. Pausing only to learn the last leg to the finish line I knew I was within reach of, I just moved.

It wasn't until the buzzer signaled the end, I realized it was the first sound my brain had heard in 3 minutes.

For the first time in my life the voices in my head shut up, and physically hurting my partner wasn't a care, concern, or cost. I just did what my partners had just taught me to do.

A cold, clear, and concentrated smile curled in my heart. Not the warm and fuzzy glowing grin my heart knows so well.

"If you were in a fight, I'd be more afraid of you than of them," Shelby said. My jaw dropped as my heart soared.

I had hit a milestone. Words I'd dared not hope to hear for months traveled backwards and forwards in time to greet me with an enthusiastic welcoming.

For the first time in my life I felt like a fighter. A real fighter, who could stand her ground and fight back.

I wanted to cry; retrospect says I should have as the moment was worth the expression. Next time. There will be a next time. I am so so so happy. Feels like I'm skydiving upside down. I think you call that soaring. Life is intense, and funny.

As always God had to put sprinkles on today's cake and icing: I'm wearing the shirt I got skydiving.

Mic drop.

I told Allen I'm afraid I won't overcome my fear of not fighting back until I'm attacked in real life.

He said, "Fear is the emotional response, being afraid is the action. All you have to do is change the action."

Why am I so afraid? I know I can take a hit; I've done it many times. I have control over my response.

"This is going to take a lot longer than I thought, isn't it?" Allen's eyes looked up from the whiteboard he was writing on.

"Facing your dragon is only the halfway point. The other half is mastering yourself."

3 hours of classes, 2 hours of free rolling, and one hot shower later, the steam cleared to reveal my own epiphany: I didn't have to "win" my real life fights, I just wanted to give it my all. Staying alive is the win. It's all up to me. I can choose to win, now.

TRIGGER WARNING
2.5
What does the Love Say on my Wedding Day?
Dear Diary,

I took out a loan to pay for our wedding. Don't tell Dave Ramsey.

I cried that morning. Sad tears. Not happy. 2 years together and I already had plenty of evidence and reasons to leave. Number two was his insistence we not get a marriage license. He was protecting me from old debts, he said. I believed him. I shouldn't have.

In the bathroom of my brother's apartment, coffee steam mixing in with the shower steam, I cried.

I stared at my blurring reflection. Questions darted across my mind like poison-tipped Cupid's arrows. Is this what I want? If he doesn't stop, can I live this life, until death do us part? What if he hurts me even worse? Is this as good as love gets? What about babies? What if he starts hurting them too? That thought brought a sob bursting through my lips. Not the babies. I can handle it, but God forbid he... I would....

"Why are you living this?" God gently asked.

"I love him. I have to live with whatever direction he goes in. I chose him, he makes his own choices, he's just making bad ones right now," my heart confessed.

"You don't deserve this. You are stronger than the victim. You are brave My Daughter. You just don't see it. You can walk away from this. It's not too late."

"Yes, it is. I love him, I've committed to this. I'm not a runaway Bride. I'd look like a fool for leaving."

"If they knew what was really happening, do you really think they'd think that?"

My head and heart dropped as the truth of His words covered me like a weighted blanket. He was right, and I knew it.

I knew it was a mistake. My head, my heart, and everything in between knew it.

"What would 8-year-old Leslie think of this fairytale?" God prodded.

"Don't go there God!" I shouted within myself. *"I'm not her anymore! I've learned. There is good in him. I see it every time he gives his testimony, and in the little things he does. That's the man I want. It's there, in him, he just doesn't see it yet. If I keep praying, keep loving him, keep holding on, I believe my happy ending will come."*

"Does it include a loaded gun pointed to his head?" God asked bold-faced.

The memories flashed across my mind like lightning. My fingers gripped the sink to keep from falling. Elbows and knees locked, heartache and tremors shook my body. The dark scar over my wounds ripped open in the light of the truth of His words.

My Beast had wanted me to suicide him. More than once. His hand held a gun to his head, sometimes his hand on the trigger, sometimes he held mine. I stood, terrified to move, unfamiliar with the safety of guns. Terrified with one wrong move, I'd lose him.

The words he shouted were coated in arsenic. He blamed me for everything. From the violent man he'd become, to his dwindling small business, even the death of his dad. He pinned every blame on my ass. I knew it wasn't true. But it was hurtful. I cried and begged him to stop. He would either continue in his blame game, or his vibes and his eyes would change, he'd pull the gun away, and laugh at me for believing he would actually do it. There was no way to win his game. Once, in dead-end desperation, I told him to go ahead and do what he wanted to. I didn't know what else to say or do. "You don't love me!" he fired back.

I was an empty shell. I had no words. No rebuttal. No argument. No twisted reason. No contextualized wording. Nothing but knowing love doesn't say or do that.

But he did.

Mind fuck.

My life was a nightmare. Yet there I was, about to play pretend fairytale wedding.

I could tell you all the cons my mind listed that morning, but that would turn this book into a burn book, and I don't want to do that. So, I'll move on to the next reason for my tears: my Dad.

Round 2 of tears hit when I thought of the memories with my dad, I'd never have. My dad wasn't going to walk me down the aisle, wasn't going to give me away, wasn't going to dance with me to songs about butterflies and kisses, because he wasn't there. The most precious moments I'd always wanted with my dad, I wasn't ever going to have.

He was standing up for his beliefs, which judged me guilty. Guilty by reason of my dress was white, but my womanhood wasn't. "I'm not walking a liar down the aisle," he said. I'd long since taken off my purity ring, in all honesty. But I still thought, to him, I was worth more than my virginity. He saw me as guilty, more than he saw me as his daughter.

I had dreamed about our daddy daughter wedding dance since dancing on his shoes as a little girl. Since dancing at the talent show. I didn't know, that was as close as I'd ever get to dancing with daddy at my wedding. The morning of my pretend wedding, I felt more unloved by him, than I ever had been. He didn't love me enough to give me away.

Prince Charming, and my earthly dad, when they looked at me, both said, "Guilty." God said, "Mine."

I could tell you all the details of those scenes my mind played that morning, but that would turn this entry into a sob story. It's enough of a pity party already. So I'll move on to a happy ending: When my 2 youngest brothers looked at me, they said, "Ours." A brother on each arm, they loved me enough to give me away. One of my favorite moments of the day.

My coffee was still hot, as I wiped my tears away. So many thoughts, so little time.

I then put on the bravest and fakest smile I had ever worn. But if you look at my pictures, you can see the lie in my eyes.

Some dreams and fairytales come true, others we lose due to the choices of people we cannot convince or control.

The wedding was for me and for show, but those daddy daughter moments would have been real.

2.6

Trickles and Tears

Dear Diary,

I tried to understand him, my dad. I tried to figure out what in his life shaped him. From my perspective he appeared to be a classic example of someone who bottled and boxed his pain, always defending and deflecting anything that comes his way. From my experience, people who do that, am doing so to protect unhealed wounds they don't want to face.

His generation, Baby Boomers, are complicated, to say the least. In my life and experiences, the men, are typically, not very nice, and the women have hearts of gold. Lost in the shadow of their military parents, they struggle to find the limelight. Neither set of my grandparents were military, but the generational attitude my parents grew up around, rubbed off on them.

The Baby Boomer men, I believe, are subconsciously demanding and expecting the same level of respect, their military fathers, earned. "Because I said so!" prevailed as an acceptable reason. Baby Boomers didn't break in bootcamp. They didn't push through the pain, toils, and trials aimed to purge the worst, and bring out the best. They didn't give it all, they didn't risk it all. They lived the American Dream their daddies paid for.

The Baby Boomer women, I believe, by watching and learning, learned how to love, when love hurt. Their mothers played both roles when they didn't know if their husbands, brothers, and fathers, would ever come home. Behind smiling faces, the mothers hid their tears, as the little girls, watched and learned through the years.

Birthed off of the industrial revolution, Baby Boomers received the benefits, without sweating the price. Life at home, became better, easier, and more comfortable and convenient. Cars, microwaves, refrigerators, appliances, most people could finally afford them. Life was good for Baby Boomers, or at least it looks good to me in all the pictures I've seen.

But if you look a little deeper, you'll see the price.

Everything was the same. Everyone had the same microwave that lasted 20 years. I remember when the brown one my mom had, had to be replaced. Variety had yet to find its way into the industry.

I believe this caused a toxic mentality, for the Baby Boomers: everything, and everyone, must be the same. For them, that was equality.

Baby Boomers struggle with change. Break the mold or break the rules and you'll be swept under the same rug everyone else has. Eventually the rug rises, no longer able to hide what's underneath and what's inside. Now what are you going to do, Baby Boomer?

My generation, watched and learned. We are the generation with the "Coexist" bumper stickers. We are advocates for therapy and personal growth. We saw the house-box our parents grew up in, turn into a prison. We love all of our men in skirts, women in leadership, crystal wearing, Christians are getting tattoos, kiss whoever you want it's all love in the end friends we have accepted as family. Love doesn't fit in a box.

If Baby Boomers had spent as much time fussing to a therapist as they did at the supper table, maybe they would have better been able to pursue happiness.

2.7

Benefit of Belief

Dear Diary,

When I look at my dad, I see desire. A desire to be recognized. Title him what you will, from entertainer to insecure, he is who he is.

I believe my dad wants what he believes is best for me. I believe he wants me to succeed. I believe he has good intentions.

What I don't trust, is his perspective. I've tried my whole life to get him to see my side, but he refuses. With many words he let me know his opinion of my fractured ribs I received as a result of Jiu Jitsu. My words saying injury is expected and unavoidable in a full contact sport, fell on deaf ears. He refused to see the gain from my pain.

I believe Baby Boomers don't know how to handle pain. If the depictions in books and movies are accurate, they learned there are two places for pain: in the bottom of a bottle or under the rug. Their veteran fathers saw a nightmare side of life, in a time where help was just a hand. Help hadn't reached the mind like it has in this time of life. Alcohol was the only medicine they had, that I know of. Their wives had to learn how to handle the man the war had made. How to handle his triggers, his nightmares, his pain. Unable to find words for what was happening as PTSD had yet to be discovered or put in the dictionary, it was better to slide on a smile and not say a thing. Sweep it under the rug and it disappears. Is it really there?

At best, my dad gives and tries his best, to what he believes in and loves. At worst, at least, the way I see it, my dad fell prey to what time teaches those who hide their pain: it finds a way out, in some way. Though that's not a story that needs to be told.

2.8

Homeplate

Dear Diary,

I went back to where it all started, my Ernie Reyes World Martial Arts school in my hometown. My old stomping grounds. It felt firm and happy. Like reading an old favorite book. Roots taken hold, lessons were learned, and now the branches have spread to Allen to finish the story.

Sweet memories swam through my mind as I wandered the red carpeted floor. The frame was still the same, but the banners and words on the walls had changed. New names of Black Belts, new mantras and ideas. The same old familiar feeling. I told the head instructor, KJN David about my book. He smiled.

His beautiful wife Sandy invited me to take the women's kickboxing class. I did. It felt so good to be back on that floor again. The floor felt the same, but I felt different. I understood what the training meant, where it went, and what the bad guy's face looked like.

My Beast used to make fun of me for never finishing things: projects, organizing, energy drinks. I just never wanted the enjoyment to be over. He was right. I give up before the end. I bail. Because I'm scared.

KJN David, saw that in me one day. I was in the backroom after class one night, practicing my one trick: the butterfly kick. Unusual for him, David came to watch. I got shy. I stopped. Typical me, I hid behind my questions.

"KJN David, why am I having so much trouble getting the butterfly kick right? I did one perfect one recently. I remember how fluid it felt, but I've not been able to copy or find it again. I'm so frustrated."

"Go do another," he solemnly said. My nerves went on overdrive. I wasn't ready to show him yet, but you don't say no to KJN David.

I stood in my stance.

"Remember how the perfect one felt. Remember every step. How it felt from start to finish, and do it," he said.

In my mind I went back to that moment. Feet firm on the red carpet. Mirror watching me in front. A few kids were playing behind me.

Step by step I remembered.

"Now do it," he said again.

I began to move, imagining my body filling in the lines like a body flash left behind by the one perfect kick. It flowed, until I doubted myself.

I failed at the end. I lost it. I panicked that it was too good to be true.

"You bailed." 2 words, 9 letters, he pinned my excuse to my ass.

I was stunned. How did he see that? It felt right, up until the last bit. Then I got scared.

I don't finish things. I find excuses to take second place and call it humility. Living vicariously in the smiles of the victorious.

Because I'm scared.

2.10

First Tap

Dear Diary,

I got my first tap today! An Americano from side control! I'm not sure how I did it, but I did!

I am so happy I'm going to cry happy tears!

2.12

First High

Dear Diary,

I'm about to go into my gym high on weed for the first time and see where my mind takes me.

Disclaimer: While the rest of the book has been edited from the original writing, this day I'm not going to. What you're about to read is raw truth. I'll edit certain parts for clarity, but the rest I'm leaving alone. You're going to see questions, yo-yo decisions and directions, enough judgement to make you (and myself) want to puke, squirrels for days, and an ugly side of Leslie. I thought about cutting this day out completely, out of pure shame. You'll soon see why. But I'm choosing not to. Here, am I, high.

I want to be free. I want to feel as high and humble as I did skydiving for my birthday after he left. The world was so big, yet I was cradled. The air I was falling against held me, it didn't fight me.

I'm excited, nervous, but feel, know, I'm in the right place. I'm about to feel, see, experience, something new. In a very safe place. This may be my last time smoking. No reason for it to, but the winds of life are shifting, strong enough for me to be lifted, and fly.

I want Allen to choke me like Beast did. I want to trap his arms, step in big circle, elbow to the face, slide step back, front kick and recover, like I should have, all those times.

Here goes, one of the best days of my life.

He doesn't have the time.

"Interesting twist," I said aloud.

Spoken often in Jiu Jitsu, my lips repeated, "Where do I go from here?"

I feel like I did smoke a little too much. I can't fake normal very easily from here. I'm still a homebody smoker. I feel scared.

But I shouldn't be. Logically speaking I have 4 hours before I have to be around people. 4 hours to come down. This is a safe space to be.

I wonder if he knows I'm high.

I just asked him for (1) 3-minute roll, just to feel things out, with my new mindset. I think he understood what I'm after. But again, he does not have the time.

I think deciding if the risk is worth the fighting off fears, comes down to this: if the end result is a bigger firework than the attacks are explosions, do it. Balance is needed, but even a spaceship uses the earth as a springboard in an effort to both leave it, and broaden its own world. You have to leave something behind, in order to get something new. Even if it's only a footprint. The earth loses the ship, but it carries very special people. Some of the world's finest. Their lives have been spent, to give home Earth, a new door.

What's worth the costs? What could possibly be as all-encompassing as pain? What else touches all areas of life from the inside to the outside?

Love is the obvious answer. But do we let it in every area of our lives or do we box it in, give it out to the areas, and people, we deem as worth our love? If love truly is the greatest treasure, why are we so greedy with it?

Why are walls what we give people who haven't even hurt us?

Walls are built to keep things in. Focusing inward first, outward to the unknown second. Men don't start fighting until after the women and children are safe. If they do, it's just because they haven't found something, or someone, they love and need to protect. Some people live their whole lives this way. Fighting against everything and everyone, because they allow no one past their wall of pain.

Yet some are a firework, birthing and bursting hope for others with freely given love. We all know what those people feel like. They are magnetic.

Some people find something or someone to love, after life takes a bite of their heart. Something, or someone has to fill it. Those that don't, those that tighten and scar it with themselves, become grumpy butts.

30 minutes ago, I would have told you when I roll with Allen I just want to fight back. Get rid of my fucking plan, and just respond to his attacks with my own.

I think now I should make the first move. Despite not knowing where I'm going, at least make my own footsteps. Explore what I don't know. Feel what happens to the world when I make the first decision. My heart just fluttered writing that. There is something behind that.

I'm coming down. Maybe a little too far down. I don't want to need or want to smoke again. I was so nervous. I want to swim in this for a while.

Prydacted's playlist is perfect for this day. It's like techno meets reggae. Pumping but calm, and no words you really have to pay attention to. I bet Channing Tatum would dance in a bowtie to some of these songs.

My heart is pounding in a bit of fear again. Sitting here on the couch right inside the door. Ring to my right, bags to my left, exercise equipment in front of me. Home got a second address quickly.

What if I'm using weed as a safety net? Why else would I want more? Alcohol takes away the edges as is its benefit. If you file the sharp points of life down, alcohol matters less and less. What cost does weed have? Nothing comes without a price. Balance. How much will this safety net cost me?

I know whatever I learn today, I have to reproduce sober too. Else it's fake and I'm using weed as smoky courage. It needs to be me.

What if God sometimes wants just the bare minimum? Not the best, not the most, just pennies so we are at least giving something, and putting a value on the lowest form of payment we have. You can still make a million bucks out of pennies.

I'm feeling starstruck around Allen for the first time since I came back that December afternoon. He will always be my hero. I want to be like him someday, in my own way.

I think Samurais are quiet because they are busy thinking and figuring out how to solve the problems of themselves and the world.

I think weed costs you the stability of stable footing. With your mind so far up in the clouds, exploring the bird's eye view, you lose a bit of the world you left behind. You know it's there; you know you will come down. Birds sit eventually.

You can run so fast you feel like you are flying. The ground doesn't hold you back when you're running over it. I think there is a correlation between all the kneeling God talks about in the Bible, and the verse about soaring on wings like eagles. I'm half convinced we won't have feet in heaven.

That ring, what is it? A battlefield? A Black Belt? A broken wedding ring? 8 walls I have to break out of? Captivity? A chrysalis? I don't know.

What have I done besides take from Allen? This book hasn't happened yet. I'm not rich yet, I can't buy him a car or a gym as a way to thank him. I don't have anything he wants or needs. I'm just being greedy by asking all this from him without giving anything in return. Bad manners, Leslie.

What do I do now? I want to cry. I kind of want to go back home. But even that's not mine. I don't have anywhere but here. Even my car crapped out. No home on 4 wheels there.

I just want to be chosen.

Maybe this is me needing to walk alone. Truly alone. It's how we all end up in the end. It's apparently how God wants me. No man, just me and my bunny Onyx.

Maybe Allen was right when he said yesterday, I look for answers in everyone else. I saw it as me taking bricks of life and building my own house.

I really want to cry.

What do I do now?

Why am I so sad? Because I have never felt chosen by a man. I pushed for Prince to propose. It got planned. After I moved to the mountains, he didn't want to spend time with me. I don't think he wanted me; I think he just wanted something better than what he had: loneliness.

I don't want to have to do this again. I want to get this over with. Choke and roll.

Maybe I need to pound on a bag. To what end? I don't know. I don't know where to go.

I think when you keep moving, you don't have time to be sad because you are already onto the next best thing.

I think the ending of this book will have less about Allen's answers and more about how I put them together to make a mosaic me. I'll figure it out.

Everybody's recipes for green bean casserole are different.

Maybe the question isn't "Where do I go from here?" but "What do I do?" I should know where I'm going. At least the direction if not the destination. I'm not that stupid, or am I?

Timelines happen when you draw the line.

I'm having to maintain normal far more than I hoped. There are extra people here. Is this a test? Probably.

If my mind was in a grateful mindset, I'd be happy getting anything from Allen. He could be charging me for the one on one talks, the way he is integrating my therapy into class times, and all the bullshit I'm putting him and Prydacted through. "But then we wouldn't get anything done. I'm not in it for the money. I'm in it as a contribution. I'm getting some things I want out of this. I want you to be as successful as you can with this," he answered when I asked him why he doesn't charge me extra.

I need to calm down and come down.

...

Alone, this whole day. Allen was booked, the circuit training class was the quietest yet. Afterwards I practiced with my sword. I made a breakthrough.

Cement footprints in my Leslie City.

I'd rather be able to be me freely. It's too much work to hide and pretend I'm not up in the clouds. Balance: For some it's easier to fake a smile, than accept things for what they are. It's easier to white wash the outside, instead of cleaning up the inside. All my life I've hidden because of my bedwetting. I don't want to have to do that anymore. I don't lie, unless it's to protect someone, but I do hide.

Allen didn't choose me like Mr. Miagi chose Daniel. I picked him. I'm the one who sold all but a bedroom's worth of furniture so I could pay for a gym membership instead of a storage unit. I'm the one who moved hundreds of miles back to Nashville to go to his gym. I'm the one who planned where I lived and worked to be nearby so I could train. I gave up so much to be here. And now I'm throwing a little bitch fit by wanting everything I want from him, and wanting it now. I've pushed hard for my timeline and my ideas on how to heal. Like I'm his fucking boss and not his student. He has his own ideas. He's way smarter than me. I need to be happy with what I'm getting, because it is working. I don't like this part of myself.

How do you hide tears? Maybe if I go punch a bag hard and long enough, I'll sweat enough to hide my tears. Sweat is tears in action.

...

I smoked more. I wonder if I stink. I'm a little worried. Was the walk barefoot across the parking lot enough to blow it away?

Bedwetting my whole life has created a deep fear of not wanting to stink. But I always wake up that way. Stinking. Odorous. I used to have a big box of perfume and body mists, but that got stolen. I know who did it. Did I go after them? No. Because I was scared and I saw it as a chance to let go of my safety net. A choice I regret. Another mistake to add to my mountain.

Allen learned tough love from his dad, that defying the odds, was worth whatever cost. His dad did the right thing.

Allen has improved the lives of I believe thousands of people. He deserves this book. He's too humble to write his own. If his career takes off over mine, his therapy measures work better than this book did, I'd be happy to have been part of it. Maybe this book is for his spotlight, not mine. He deserves it. I ran in fear for 30 years. He faced life head on, at 8.

I'm fighting off a seizure. I have 9 minutes to pull myself together.

Today is ending. I need to fake it till I'm in bed. Today needs to have an ending.

...

I can't cry pretty. Twice on the way home my mind hijacked my intention, and I didn't feel safe enough to cry. Too many people around at the stoplights. The risk wasn't worth it.

I feel like I've had a crash course on fear today. Like Allen said, "If you tell the Universe you are going to do something, it will test you, to make sure." This day went nothing like I hoped it would.

I need to cry and sleep. Sucks the walls are thin. I don't want my roommates to hear me.

It's the end, what do I do now?

2.14

Valentine's Day

Dear Diary,

It's Valentine's Day, and I miss him. I miss the happy times we did have. I miss the little bit of love he had for me. I miss his smile, his bright eyes, his hugs, his cuddles, I could go on and on.

My favorite memory of him is waking him for work, day after day. He worked hard, and he slept deep. The siren of his alarm rarely woke him, but my soft voice could. No matter how hungover I was, or how mad he was at me when he went to sleep, I always set my own alarm, to wake him.

His eyes would flutter, quickly, as his hunter's eyes quickly surveyed the bedroom. Scanning, to see where he was, what was going on, and who else was there. I saw confusion, mild fear, and quick assertion fly through his eyes. Until they found me.

As his eyes landed on mine, he would smile, in a hazy, still half dreaming way. He would immediately calm down. Eyes no longer looking for anything.

He loved me there.

Prince told me one of his favorite things about me, happened when I was asleep. On the off chance I was deeply asleep when he got home, he'd get into bed, and I'd begin to stir. He'd snuggle up to me, trying not to wake me. In my half-asleep state, eyes still closed, he said I would whimper. Took him a bit to figure out my whimpering was whining he wasn't close enough to me. Once he pulled me onto his chest, he said I smiled in my sleep.

I loved him so much.

"Love never dies, it just changes shape," my heart said.

"It's time to let go, Leslie," my mind said.

Ecclesiastes 3, in the KJV Bible helped me understand time and love and loss. It reads:

1) To everything there is a season, and a time to every purpose under the heaven:

2) A time to be born, and a time to die; a time to plant, and a time to pluck up that which is planted;

3) A time to kill, and a time to heal; a time to break down, and a time to build up;

4) A time to weep, and a time to laugh; a time to mourn, and a time to dance;

5) A time to cast away stones, and a time to gather stones together; a time to embrace, and a time to refrain from embracing;

6) A time to get, and a time to lose; a time to keep, and a time to cast away;

7) A time to rend, and a time to sew; a time to keep silence, and a time to speak;

8) A time to love, and a time to hate; a time of war, and a time of peace.

"It's time to let go," my heart agreed. *"Happy Valentine's Day, Leslie. Love yourself."*

2.15

Momentum

Dear Diary,

I decided to go to the gym on a Friday, out of my normal. Opportunity knocked with the chance to spar for the first time. I said yes.

"I don't want to hurt you!" I giggled and said over and over. The men played by bopping my head.

"You're the one in the ring. You're already braver than those sitting out," Chad said. I smiled.

My technique was sloppy and I couldn't get over not wanting to hurt them, but I had a blast. It was all worth it.

The first step is never a failure.

2.17
Everything is Awesome
Dear Diary,

Sometimes 'Once Upon a Time' just isn't enough for one of the best days of life. Especially when they keep running together.

The day started with a hug my heart hadn't felt in 4 years. Time sweetens the best of friends. "It's nice seeing you this happy," he said. "It's nice feeling this happy," I said. We relived the best of times in the years we'd been apart. My heart was full of warm fuzzies.

The other drivers must have thought I was loony for the smile on my face on the drive to Jiu Jitsu.

Would I get a happy ending? A new beginning? Standing at the base of the ring, God said, "Footprints."

In my mind's eye I saw an image of my life glazing over the black Jiu Jitsu mat. Like someone put a city rug over the vinyl. A map of my life. I saw people, places, paths, homes, decisions, and me, walking alone. A second set of footsteps intertwined with mine. In some places my steps veered far away from the bigger ones. Sometimes, there was only one set.

"When you see only one set of footprints," God gently whispered to my heart, "It was then that you followed Me."

I smiled so big I could see my chipmunk cheeks under my eyelashes. The image faded, and I walked onto the mat.

The class began, and the puzzle pieces fell like dominoes on the mat. The moves began to take sequence. In my mind, they began to make sense.

I smiled the whole time.

The ending move had me fighting not only my opponent, but tears of joy on the mat. One or two escaped.

Allen caught me in my first rear naked choke. Through the fears, flashbacks, and tears, I fought. Quickly, I moved his bottom leg, and slid over it before he had a chance to lock me in. As I slid, his grip on my neck, loosened as the angle changed. I was free. A tear or 2 flowed. I had fought, and I was free.

3 taps later, my day was made.

Last Sunday I had my first tap, today, I tripled that.

After class I felt led by God to drill my roundhouse kick.

WHAP! My leg kissed the bag with a sound louder than I'd heard yet.

In the same direction as the kick, like yellow tissue paper over the black floor, I saw long yellow bricks leading to a vanishing horizon. I knew I was on the right path.

WHAP WHAP WHAP over and over and over. As I pushed myself, I felt a pull from within. Like the opposite of a black hole. A never-ending supply of, I don't have a word for it. I could pull from it, to push myself. A power with purpose, light, and love.

I was loving what I was becoming capable of. I could feel God's pride soar too. He was proud of me. I could feel Him smile.

"Let it flow from within, not at the edge of the waterfall." He said as He stirred the swell in my chest into a roar. I relaxed into it, and kicked.

A new sound. Hard, but not as forced. Effortless.

WHAP WHAP WHAP over and over and over.

Like swimming in a river, I created momentum with each move.

As my body began to create momentum, my mind began to slow. Rarely have I been in places in life I wanted to stay in. Till recently. I am beginning to "enjoy the moment" as they say. Like right then. I wanted to stay. God wasn't done. Butterfly kick, the pretty and pretty useless one.

"Give me your best," He said.

I wish I could tell you it all clicked and I did amazing. I didn't. I had a hard time. 20 minutes of ebb and flow, but no dam breaking.

"Stop expecting it to feel a certain way, Leslie. What you have is enough for me."

"But I want to make you proud." He smiled. I felt it.

"Celebrate. Throw your chest out on the twist and actually look at the audience. Spread your arms like an eagle." I smiled.

I wish I could tell you it felt perfect and I broke a wall, but I can't. It felt wonderful, but a wall still stands.

Swoosh, over and over and over, trying to break the wall.

It wasn't until I believed Him, that my efforts began to feel like enough. He wasn't mad at me for not being able to do a beautiful butterfly kick. He was happy with just me.

I began to push myself. Show off for God. "Just one more," I told my tired legs. "I can do better than that one."

One turned into many, as I drilled for another 15 minutes or so. Until I felt God saying I was enough, and slightly overdoing it. He was happy with me.

He loves me no matter what I give Him.

I went to the bathroom, locked the door, knelt, and thanked Him.

Out I came to rest a bit. People seemed to find me. Doors were opening. Conversations were handed to me. A magnetism of light I felt within me. My happy was infectious and spreading like glitter. It seemed people wanted a piece of what I had. Or now have as it seems to have been planted and sprouted in recent days. I am making people smile.

Maybe this is how heroes do it.

2.20
Mitchell

Dear Diary,

I'm not sure exactly what happened today, but something big, did.

There is a blonde headed quiet guy named Mitchell in Jiu Jitsu. We started about the same time. Been progressing about the same rate. Today, we rolled together for the first time, and I submitted him. I didn't think I could, and by the looks on his and our classmates' faces, neither did they.

We did our drills, then squared up to roll. Everyone knew it was Mitchell's and mine's first time rolling together. We were being watched.

He smiled, "I guess this is it," he said. Oh no he didn't. Where the heck was his manners?! Some things you just don't say. Now it felt more like a battle than a roll. Indignation rising, I simmered, and chalked it up to him being young as he is a decade younger than me. Yes, yes, I did. I pulled the age card. Retrospect showed me I took his comment far too seriously. It was meant in good fun. I took a deep breath, let it go, and rolled.

I truly expected him to win based on strength alone. In the month I'd seen him roll, it was obvious he was naturally strong. I didn't think even my ego-pricked adrenaline could out strengthen him. He was going to win.

But I fought. As hard as I could, I fought. And I won with an Americano from side control. I was shocked. By the look on his face, so was he. By the looks on our classmates, they were too.

My pride lasted only moments. As we circled around for post class review, I watched him. The look in his eyes, and his body language, nearly broke my heart.

I saw a 20-year-old man beaten by a 30-year-old woman. I saw a young man, whose pride was broken, but he was hiding it well. He sat, his eyes shifting as his mind raced. His eyes kept flickering in thought. I wish I knew what he was thinking. His arms limply rested on his legs, like they didn't know what to do. His breathing was heavy. If it were me, I would have been crying.

The atmosphere in the room had changed. I felt the respect I had gained. But seeing Mitchell, sitting there, broken, when only minutes ago he was smiling and excited, it wasn't worth it. It wasn't worth my "win." I would have given anything to go back and let him win. To see the smile and the pride in his eyes again.

I don't mind being stepped on if I know it's helping someone step up. What he didn't know wouldn't hurt him right? Had I known my win would do this to him, I would have given it to him. This may be a convoluted way of thinking, but everyone wins this way. Someday it will be my turn.

As class ended and we bowed out, I made sure to ask him if he was ok. He smiled a half smile and said, "Yeah." He's so strong and doesn't even know it.

I feel so bad.

2.21

Ball Drop

Dear Diary,

Sitting here on the couch next to the ring writing, and Mitchell walks in. He is never here before class. His vibe is completely different. He is walking with purpose, straight to the machines I still don't know what they are used for or called. His eyes are calm, seemingly focused on something I can't see. His shoulders are back, where yesterday they slumped. He sees me, and smiles.

Earphones in, he begins to train.

He's changing.

2.22

Rinse and Repeat

Dear Diary,

Different day, same changed Mitchell. He is coming in and kicking ass.

2.24

Fire in the Mitchell

Dear Diary,

Mitchell is on fire. In a fantastic way. Here we are, only a few days after what appears to have been his rock bottom, and he is on fire.

Instead of letting the fact a 30-year-old woman beat his 20-year-old self, bust his balls, he has learned from it. It's only rock bottom if you stay there. He has used rock bottom as his launching pad. It's beautiful.

His demeanor, his drive, his focus, has all completely changed. That man is going places. He is going to compete in the ring someday. I can see it in his eyes. And he will win.

I am so proud of him. I love knowing I was a part of his growth.

I think I was wrong in thinking that giving him the win was a good idea. My mind reminded me of Allen's story about sparring the book smart guy. Allen held back the first round. "The victory smile on the student's face was paid for with a lie," Allen had said. If I had given Mitchell the win, it would have been lying. Lying to him by him believing he was getting my best, as he was giving his. It would have been cheating, cheating myself the potential win, and cheating him the honor of a true win. It would have been stealing. Stealing the validity of the moment by me manipulating the situation for what I believed to be best. Because I am "older and know better." *Insert eye roll here.* And it would have been killing, killing the potential he and I both have.

You can't grow by holding back. The next step always starts wherever you are, with whatever you have. And truth always gets found out in the end.

Had I given him the win, and he found out, God only knows how he would have felt.

I feel good.

2.25

Pay it Forward

Dear Diary,

A friend called, wanting to hang out. I went. I went for a good time, and good friendship. I got much more in return.

My friend had a bit too much of the good stuff. Soon after arriving at his house, he went to the bathroom, and stayed there. Worried, I knocked and asked if he was ok. I knew the meaning of his slurring words all too well. He was shitfaced and had fallen asleep on the toilet. He was not ok. Holding a shirt up to hide his dignity, I went in to find what I imagined I looked like, all those years I was drunk.

For the first time in my life, I got to be the one helping. I got him to finish throwing up, wiped off, and somehow managed to get clean pants on him, while maintaining his dignity. He mumbled apologies and thanks as I helped. I smiled.

The hardest part was getting him to bed. As I was not yet that strong, I couldn't simply fireman's carry him. Half an hour went by, step by step, as I shouldered his weight, and shuffled him to bed. With a few quick turnarounds back to the toilet. Nearly 2 hours had gone by since I had arrived. He was finally safe, and stable in bed. I plugged his phone in, wrote him a note, and left.

I got to take care of a friend the same way dozens of people took care of my drunk butt over the years. Finally, I got to pay it forward.

I was so happy I got that chance. I don't even care if he doesn't remember tomorrow. I know what I did. God knows too.

Full, beautiful circle.

2.26

Believe

Dear Diary,

Earlier this week, at the end of a boxing camp, I heard Allen say, "Live life believing that you're right until someone tells you you're wrong. Believing you're wrong all the time is no way to live."

They did line punches. Everyone stood, arms up, against the wall mat, and took a punch from everyone, including Allen.

At first the punches were light, playful, and excited. Allen's was always the strongest one. He knew what they could take. As the punches rolled in and the people rolled out, they grew stronger. High fives, hugs, and pats on the back, the adult version of gold stars.

Some people laughed when they got hit, some people looked a little nervous. Others kihapped. They all glowed.

The shy, and bigger guy of the group, the one whose nerves I thought would shoo him out the door the first week, took the wall. He smiled, big. Bigger than the rest. He had a smile and confidence I'd not yet seen. He was proud of himself. He took the hits like a man, smiling, laughing, and growing in confidence a mere 30 feet away. His smile brought tears to my eyes. 5 weeks had taken him from nervous, to Knight.

Allen took the wall. He smacked his torso, let out a rallying cry, and let them go. As the punches grew in strength, so did his kihaps. It was empowering to watch.

After their class ended, I walked over to the now confident guy, and told him everything I just wrote. How I have watched, from the couch, the change in him. How I was so proud of him. His smile grew bigger and bigger. It was the beginning of a sweet friendship.

His name is Hunter.

2.27

Fear, Failure, and Friends

Dear Diary,

I asked God what my fear was, and He answered: not being wanted.

I had to make a choice, and I made the wrong one, today. I made the choice to depend on other people for my next step. When they didn't do what I wanted them to do, I threw a massive internal pity party, until Allen told me what to do. Embarrassment, crashed my party, as I knew, I should have known.

"It's my party, I'll cry if I want to," my heart said.

"Three person teams," Allen said.

"Choose yourself, Leslie," my mind said.

The one guy to swoop in and "save the day," was the last one I expected. A guy who all I knew, was his name: Frank. I joined him and his friend for what was left of the drills.

Free rolling began.

A few rough neck grabs in free rolls had me fighting to stay conscious. I nearly bowed out. But bowing out meant failure, so I pushed on through the waves of darkness to find the light.

"Is it over yet?" my heart cried.

The silent tick of the timer, said no.

"Bowing out isn't failure, Leslie," my mind said.

My last roll was with the sweetheart Frank. Thank God. He was skinny, but strong. No pressure, no fear.

We played it safe, comfortable, until in the last 30 seconds Allen said, "Make something happen guys."

On our knees, I swept his leg and mounted.

"Good Leslie!" he sincerely said. I smiled through the tears his sweetness had brought to my eyes.

"Happy endings do happen," my heart sighed.

"Happy endings happen when you make them happen," my mind said.

"I agree," I said.

MARCH 10 STEPS

March 1st
Dizzy in the Middle
Dear Diary,
    I met a soccer mom whose husband was trying the boxing class, and whose adorable son was playing nearby. Pleasantries opened a door as to why I was there. I began my usual spiel, but my mind reminded me it needed to change. I tripped over my words as they came out.
    "My husband, well, actually, technically my boyfriend because he didn't want a marriage license…"
    "I was a victim, I mean, a survivor of domestic violence."
    "I'm here to learn better how to defend myself. I mean fight my fear. I mean fight my dragon. I mean make a stronger me."
    "Geez Leslie, will you listen to yourself?" my heart chided.
    "I'm just here for fuel. I'm really not interested in all the drama," she said.
    "Don't get your panties in a wad. She can't see the change you are making on the inside," my mind chipped.
    She walked away to fix her son's already perfect hair. I was left in the mess my good intentions had made.
    "Now what?" my heart asked, dejectedly.
    The sound of bags being hit, filled the gym.
    "Make your next move," my mind directed.
    I waited for an opportune moment, and began chatting with her again. Asked her for her story, she responded, and warmed.
    The conversation was cut short by the opportunity to spar with a friend. "One of my favorite parts of my week!" I said. She smiled.
    Perspective changes everything. What to her was a wall of unnecessary information that made me look unstable at best, crazy at worst, was an open door in the right direction for me. It's never too late to rewrite the middle to create a better ending.

3.3
Wake Up and See the Stars
Dear Diary,

This week has been hard. Work groove, period hormones, feeling lonely, my mind slowly changing, has made me a mess. But I'm trying.

Shelby was my last round in today's Jiu Jitsu class. I grinned and said, "Now I get to show you all the stuff I've learned."

He smiled, "Alright, I'm excited to see."

"Don't go easy on me," I said. We rolled. It was a blast. A solid fist bump and a proud grin ended the match.

"You're definitely better." My heart soared.

I asked him to stick around and watch me box as I had learned things there too. He did.

Boxing is where it happened.

The story I couldn't see was Lucas and Shelby talking. They knew I was being hit like a girl, and someone needed to teach me a lesson.

After 6 rounds Allen boxed with me. Our first time. Slow at first, feeling things out, then BAM! He hooked me as my hands came down.

I saw stars for the first time.

"He hurt me!" my heart cried.

THUD my knees hit the black mat.

"He hit you," my mind said.

Tears welled behind my eyes as my ego threw a hissy fit. I knew there was good intent behind the hit, but it still hurt my feelings.

"Whoa!" I moaned in shock and weird head pain.

He was laughing. Not in a mean way, but in a "I've been there too," and "You've just been initiated," way.

"You ok?" he asked, with a caring and knowing tone.

Wake up call. I had to get up. I panted as I stood up on wobbly legs. Tears filling my eyes, head pounding, and little blurry comet tails still trailing across my vision. I took my stance.

I forget what I said but I remember his response was, "Yeah, it's hard to push through." The rest of the round is a blurry memory.

His words hit me with the last punch: "Don't rely on someone else to protect you." His point pierced through the bullseye of my heart to the floor beneath my Achilles' heel. He had found it. Tears flooded my eyes in an attempt to put out the flames of fear coursing through my body. "Keep your guard up and don't let them in. You have to protect yourself," he said.

All I ever wanted was a Prince to fight for me, protect me, treasure me. I never wanted to see the dragon. Never wanted to be the hero.

I was taught from an early age monsters lay outside, in "The World." That's what I was taught. Everything not of God was of the world and equally of the Devil. Movies with magic were rarely allowed in my house. My friend didn't have any dolls with boobies. Spaghetti strap shirts were slutty, and on the radio only soft oldies and Christian music played. I didn't grow up in a cult, but I did grow up with a very judgmental and narrow-minded view of the world outside my home and church. A world boxed in by fear that only gaining a husband could take away. A woman's place was in the home and under the wing of her husband.

I love having little brothers, but I always wanted a big brother. I never wanted to be the strong one. I wanted someone to give me piggyback rides, advice, a man for me to sit beneath his protective wing.

Yet there I was, in the ring, fighting, for myself.

"I'm sorry I had to do this for your training Leslie, but it's part of the process. You have to grow," Allen said. I just tried to keep standing.

"I didn't get up fast enough," I said later, as my tears and insecurities began to flow.

"What matters is that you did. Do you now feel the difference in the punches? Those guys were being nice. I was being real."

I did. I felt it. I didn't mind it, but my body did. My sore neck told me I can't take a headshot. I will have to ask my chiropractor about the risk.

Until then, my head is spinning, both physically dizzy and waking up to a new reality. I'm not sure which way is up.

3.4
Reality's Dream
Dear Diary,

    I was 8-years-old, when I found my dream in my reality.

    At that time, church to me was a place I got to wear a pretty dress, people sat in "ladders" as I called them. Not knowing what pews were called, to me the shape was the same. A man would get up on stage, talk for a while, and people left with a smile. Happier than when they came in. I liked it. I later learned, as it was a Southern Baptist church, the smile came from the pat on the back the sermon gave them.

    One day, things changed. My Sunday best dress was on, my family went to what looked like a church to me. A cross hung above the stage; colorful windows lined the hallways. But the lines were different. Instead of "ladders" of happy people, there was one long line of sad people, and little circles of people talking and crying. Everyone was crying. At 8-years-old, I didn't understand why. I thought this was supposed to be a happy place.

    It looked like things were going back to normal, after we all went to another room where we sat in the "ladders." A man got up on stage, and I thought things were going to get better. He talked, and everyone cried harder. I was so confused and didn't know what to do.

    I decided, right then and there, I wanted to be the other man. The one who got up on stage and with his words made everyone smile. I liked the ripple effect I saw and understood one person could do. My dream awoke that day.

    It wasn't until years later, when I finally understood, the sad place, was the funeral of my Uncle Wally, a WW2 Veteran.

    At age 10, I began writing.

    Smiles are the other half of a rainbow.

3.5
What a Beautiful World
Dear Diary,

    I was 12 years old, when the combination of learning what a Bucket List was, crime drama television, and a short story, added up to one of the best decisions I have ever continued to make.

At the top of my Bucket List was "Save a life." I don't know why. I imagined a theatrical save from a drowning or a house fire, though I wasn't a strong swimmer. Or maybe I'd stop a mugger or kidnapper in the streets, like I'd seen on crime drama tv.

A short story, changed my mind. I read a story of a 14-year-old girl, who had had enough of life. One morning she awoke, to what she decided, was going to be her last sunrise. She dressed in black, went to school, and hatched her suicide plan. A ray of sunlight, changed her mind. Someone, somewhere, noticed her out of the blue. They said something nice to her, something she wasn't used to. I can't remember what the compliment was, but I do know it was enough to change her mind. She didn't take her life that night. One small sentence, saved her life.

How to save a life, was that easy. Easy as speaking a few happy words. I decided I could do that.

I began to look for opportunity, for the beauty, in "The World." Beauty on women and girls. Pretty hair, a pretty dress, pretty shoes, anything would do. I remember being in 5th grade Sunday school, asking for the pretty girls to be my bathroom buddies. One by one, I nervously and shyly told them I thought they were pretty. A chorus singing "aww" and a smile, was often their reply. I just wanted to make their lives happier.

Next up were the mothers checking books out of the library where I volunteered. They often wore shiny jewelry, and loved to tell me the story behind their charms.

As time and myself grew, my understanding of what I was doing, deepened. At first, I just loved seeing the smiles I got in return for my complimentary words. The smiles lit up their faces on an otherwise normal day. And they stayed. Their smiles stayed on their faces far longer than it took the compliment to come out of my mouth. A great return on investment. I should have been on Wall Street. Kidding, kind of.

It wasn't just the smiles I saw. I felt a change in the air between me and them. It seemed to sparkle. Retrospect told me it was the ice melting. I still believe it's magic.

I'm not going to tell you the other things I did to make people smile, because that would be bragging. Suffice to say I learned who needed the compliments: the mother at the grocery store whose 4-year-old girl and 2-year-old boy running up and down the aisles of produce, fascinated by the colors, needed it. Wonder filled their eyes, fear filled hers. She was fearful someone would think her children were ill-behaved. "Your kids are so cute!" wiped her fear from her face. Women like her, teens wearing black, and wallflowers lost in the shadows, I saw, I said, they smiled.

As the world of those around me brightened with smiles, the world I was taught to fear, became beautiful. The more I looked for beauty, the more I found. I learned those without crosses around their necks, and Bibles in their hands, were nice people. I saw nothing and no one to be afraid of. I began to yearn to be a part of "The World" that made such wonderful people and things. It wasn't so bad after all.

I won't know until I die, if these 20 years of raining sweet compliments like a candy queen, will have saved a life. But I do dream. I dream of my first day in heaven, and a 100-year-old woman walks up to me, and smiles.

3.6
Too Far
Dear Diary,

I smoked too much weed before class. I'm scared. I don't like what this has done to my mind.

What if my rapist walked into Jiu Jitsu and I had to free roll with him? What would I do? Attack? Submit? Tell Allen? Act out my best lie as though everything was fine?

I'm scared. This is not where I need to be.

3.7
Plans
Dear Diary,

I told Allen I need something to happen on the anniversary of my unhappy ending, July 4th. I need us to do something. But he gets to choose because he obviously knows best.

I don't know where I'll be at that point, but I know I need a line drawn, a breakthrough, breakaway, something, to change. I'm still mourning and I know it. Warm piles of unfolded laundry cannot fill the emptiness of my cold bed. It's been almost 2 years, I want this pain to end.

Why the fuck do I miss someone that hurt me so much?

3.8
The Last Shot
Dear Diary,
It was after our unhappy ending, when my Beast tried, for the last time, to hit me again. The times and our lives were now different, so was his attempt. I say attempt, because for the first time, I stopped it. Stopped not an object, but for one of the few times, it was his actual hand.

He'd slapped me across my face and my body, in the past. One of the only ways he would make direct contact.

We were standing in the dark hallway arguing about what I don't remember. His arm began to raise, before it could hit my face, I caught it with my palms, the way I had been trained. I flung it away from me.

"Don't you ever touch me like that again!" I said in a tone as hard and cold as dry ice.

His eyebrows raised, his mouth smiled a little, as it so often did. His amused eyes said, "Well, well, well, little bitch."

I spun on my heel and walked away before he could swing or say anything again.

To this day I don't know why he didn't follow me, or try again.

I do know why I stopped him.
I was no longer his. I was mine.

3.10
The Gift
Dear Diary,
Free rolling gave me a few taps, and the best roll I've ever had with Mitchell.

"Show me what you got," I said. He smiled. He was more secure, still strong, but without something to prove. I got the set up for the triangle from the drills we learned, and he slowed down.

"Find it," he said. He was being kind. In all his training he had surpassed me in Jiu Jitsu, we both knew it. But I was ok with that. My time will come.

As I was about to clinch the triangle he started fighting back.

"This feels right," my heart said.
"I'm not giving it to you," Mitchell grinned and said.
"That's how Jiu Jitsu rolls," my mind said.

End of class philosophy talk landed Allen's eyes on mine as he said, "When you get hit over and over eventually you see it coming from a mile away."

A later talk with Shelby revealed my bad boxing. The Sunday I was hit by Allen, it was noticed by everyone but me, that I wasn't keeping my hands up.

Shelby and Lucas, the spider monkey fighter, watched and talked. "I'm about to get my gloves and go in there and do it for her myself," Shelby said to Lucas. Allen walked in and did it himself.

I was being hit like I was a girl. Everyone but me saw it. Shelby also reminded me it was ok to cry, but if I do, to keep my head up, and look them in the eye because it's nothing to be ashamed of. I want to cry, I need to cry, but I haven't found a safe enough place to yet. I'm still afraid.

A private talk with Allen taught me perfection is the goal, but it cannot be attained. I need to ride the wake, not the wave. To let go so I can be in the next moment. And to get out of my head and into my senses. The brain can't see, hear, smell, taste, or touch, it only interprets what it absorbs. I need to trust what I know.

Praying to God in the shower later, He told me this: "Bow to no one but Me. It's not martyrdom when you don't fight. I died to give you life, fight to keep it." I leaned onto the warming shower wall, and cried.

3.11
Like a Child
Dear Diary,

Where do you go when you aren't sure where the next step is?

Coach T was in the ring sparring with a 6-year-old kid with the energy of a 2-year-old. I watched.

The child's movement caught my eye. He was fluid, not fighting. The child stretched from within, not up to a standard. Like a rubber band stretching outward as far as it could, then falling back to its original shape. As soon as his little gloves hit the pad, he came back to his stance, never taking his eyes off Coach-T. He was relaxed, but strong. It was beautiful.

"Go train on the bags," God said. I put my laptop up, and raised my gloves. I stepped, left foot forward. Power side in front. Normally I'm southpaw, but today I felt like trying new things. Punch. Punch. Punch. I smiled. I felt strong.

Boxing techniques class began, Allen, Coach T, and 2 other people. We worked on base stance and footwork. My left foot forward. Trying out my new stance.

It wasn't long before I realized Allen must have seen me train on my own and switch from southpaw. He was covering all the bases, basics, and punches. Letting me explore.

Punches 1-8 were next on the pads. Foot work, steps, pivots, shoulder rotations, recoils, it felt better with my stronger side in front. I got excited and began to rush the punches, and got sloppy. Allen caught me and pulled me in to focus. On my 6th punch, right uppercut, I landed a solid hit. His eyes sparked. "There ya go!" I was catching on. On the 8th punch, liver shot, I felt the natural pivot of my body, and glided. His eyes lit up and held the light of knowledge of something I couldn't see. I smiled.

Coach T and I got to work together. We fell into a rhythm. His smile held a bit of fun, excitement, and the pride of seeing his work with me bloom. He was my coach too.

Coach T and I trained one on one in the ring after class. My stance was better, I felt more protected, and my combos began to sync. 20 minutes in I landed my longest combo, 17 moves in a row. I'm happy with that ending.

3.13
Broke but not Beat
Dear Diary,

"Are yall going to fight?" asked a fellow classmate. As a guy named Blake and I, entered the ring.

"Yes," yes, I was going to fight. From dancing in my bedroom alone to sparring with a friend. I was going to fight. I felt fabulous. We sparred, the guy watched, and I felt like a star.

Odd woman out in Jiu Jitsu, we paired off for rear naked chokes from backpack. Fear pierced my heart like an arrow. This battle still rages.

I was told by Allen to pair with sweet Frank and his friend. Instead of sitting and watching, I copied the moves as they drilled, making it work on my own.

I saw a better opportunity with Mitchell and the new guy, Noah. Their drills finished, I asked Mitchell if I could drill with him. I made my own way.

Free rolling began. I claimed Mitchell for a 5-minute round. Made my own decision. It's so much fun watching his growth. He is still better than me at this point. The fire in him has created a newfound beast mode. I'm a late bloomer, but I'll find mine eventually.

Noah freaked me out. He is crazy strong. He has a kill shot, must have been a wrestler or street fighter. His arm found a home under my chin every time I lifted my head. His elbows found my nose a few times. I had to fight to stay safe as his fighting style was not the safe, smooth, technical way Allen teaches. It was kill shots. It hurt.

It brought me back to my Beast. My Beast fought me this way. I panicked. Fear flooded my veins. Flashbacks flooded my mind. I wanted to cry. I wanted to walk out. But I had to hold on. His armbar caught me. I tapped too late. My elbow ached. Panic still ran in my veins. Finally, the roll was over. I trembled.

"This is too much," my heart said.

"Switch partners," Allen said.

"It won't last forever," my mind said.

Mitchell was next. Thank God. He was safe. My fear dissipated and was replaced by excitement. Rinse and repeat I found the rear naked choke. Smiling, he fought me harder, as he broke past my leg, and got out of it.

"Nothing comes free," Allen laughed as he walked by. I smiled.

Frank's friend caught me in another armbar. I saw lightning across my eyes. Paused.

"You need a rest?" he kindly asked.

Realizing I was losing control of myself, I shook off the pain and focused on getting back in the roll.

"I'm good."

It wasn't until we stood to bow out that I felt the stab of broken bone and saw the flashback: I had broken my right big toe midroll with Mitchell. I remembered being on the floor as I tried to sweep him from under his mount. But I planted my foot wrong, and had broken it. Adrenaline subsiding, the pain, and the color purple, was now obvious. Spoiler alert: a future x-ray would show the same bone in both feet behind my big toes, were and still are dislocated, not broken. I may need surgery someday.

"Nice job on staying tough," Allen said. I wondered what he saw. I smiled.

I love this.

3.14
Steps and Threads
Dear Diary,

Circuit training was hard with my foot pain, but I managed around it. Found out I have strong obliques. Had the best number in the class for oblique crunches, and wasn't sore or tired.

Allen told me I spar like I'm moving on stilts. Frustrated, I lowered my stance and remembered I have knees. One step at a time.

I fumbled when I sparred Allen. My guard was lost, I overthought, and I couldn't focus. I was sloppy. He's my hero but along with that comes intimidation. Not because of him, but because my self-esteem is so low.

On the way home, tears and prayers finally fell.

"Trust Me, trust yourself. You know what to do. The answers are already within you," said God.

A bridge starts with a thread. A thread of hope. I'm trying to make every step solid gold before I build the next. But I don't know where I'm going.

3.16
Love Language
Dear Diary,

My nursery as a baby was done in rainbows. I've ever since held on to rainbows as a love language between me and God. Whenever I'm sad and need to actually see Him, I'll ask for one. He always delivers. Today's was funny.

Self-esteem beating me like a bully, and period hormones turning me into a cry baby, I cried and prayed for a rainbow as I left the store.

"Look to your left, Leslie," God said.
The word "Rainbow" lit a store front. A literal answer to my prayer. I laughed.
"Go in, Leslie," He said. I laughed, and I did.
I found myself in a wonderland. Glitter and rainbows were on everything: dresses, purses, shoes, makeup kits, even the floor. It was beautiful. I wandered through the wonderland, and thanked God over and over again.
I adulted and only bought workout shirts and 1 glittery handbag. It had a rainbow on it, of course.
Thank God, for literally answered prayers.

3.17
Scared and Sad
Dear Diary,
My body is busted. I'm severely dehydrated, I'm ill from medical issues I don't want to talk about, and my feet hurt with every step.
Rear naked choke, again. I am so fucking scared. I think the difference in a demon and a dragon, is position and perspective. A demon hovers over your shoulder, like a dark cloud or shadow. Looming, threatening, and whispering in your ear. When you turn and face the demon, it becomes a dragon, a dragon you can fight.
I feel like I've spent my whole life looking over my shoulder. Waiting to be yelled at, waiting for Prince Charming to show up and fix everything, waiting for someone to find my secret shame. I have ducked and covered, my whole life. My chiropractor even has the x-rays to prove it. My neck curves forward in a way it shouldn't. Time and traction will fix it. He fixes everything else I knock out in Jiu Jitsu. I literally could not do it without him.
Can you tell I'm sad today?

3.18
Rainbow Round 2
Dear Diary,
"When you believe everything has a reason, nothing you do is a mistake," God said in our morning chat.
A coworker got told she was the sunshine of the office. That's usually my title. Ego bruised, I asked, "What am I then?"

"The rainbow," the woman replied. My heart soared; my face smiled.

She didn't know the meaning of what she had said, but I did. It meant God.

Later I told two girls in a weight loss camp at the gym, they could do it, just as I had. My own 60lb weight loss was hard, but worth it. A light sparkled in their eyes. They smiled. They don't know that's how I show Jesus.

In boxing class, we continued to work on stance. My timing was faster, I began to see punches ahead of impact.

Then the 3rd rainbow, lit my life. When describing the side to side movements of a slip, Allen said, "It's a rainbow." My heart pounded in my chest. Another one! God was on fire! This is how He loves me!

But God was about to out-do even Himself.

"Twist, drop, and rise," Allen said about the bob and weave. "Like a horse on a carousel." Oh, my, God. Carousels are one of my happy places. A place I get lost in the spins and golden glow of childhood magic and dreams. I even have a picture of me on one, my eyes lost in fantasy. It's beautiful.

"I love you," my heart whispered to God.

"I love you too, my dear Daughter," God spoke.

"I know You, God," my mind said.

Today was a fairytale.

3.19
The Burn
Dear Diary,

Boxing conditioning. I put my gloves on.

"For a pushup, imagine you are pushing the earth away from you, not you from the earth," Allen said. Girl pushups be done, I tried the new way he said. Suddenly the push-up came easier. The new technique made so much bodily sense. I have never done them that fast or that well. I smiled. Really big. It helped keep my head up.

The day wrapped itself in warm fuzzies with an old friend from Ernie Reyes, who like myself, found his way back to Allen. An old boyfriend of mine who was now happily married with an adorable baby boy.

I watched as Allen's eyes lit up in pride as he walked through the gym doors.

Surprise, and pride, in his voice, Allen nearly shouted his name, "Nick!" Nick grinned.

I watched, staying away as this was not the moment for a full Ernie Reyes reunion. This was their moment. I watched as the smiles, the kind that only time strengthens and deepens, stayed on their faces. They laughed, they talked, they reminisced. It was beautiful.

I wanted to, but didn't take the class. My body had had enough. I wanted to pair with Nick, have our own little reunion, but I knew I would have held him back. His skill level was far higher than mine. Bailey, one of the best women kickboxers in the gym, was up to his speed. I just smiled, watched, and lived vicariously.

3.20
Fear and Trembling
Dear Diary,

Triangle from guard review. Many movements, hard to remember them all. I avoided being put in one. I'm scared these days.

The new powerhouse Noah still scares me. He is blossoming, strong, and untamed. I asked him to keep an eye out for his elbows and my face. It didn't work. I get hit and hurt every time I roll with him. While rolling he yanked me into a tight triangle. I tapped. I knelt, breathed, and pulled myself together. I was so scared.

"Didn't hurt as much as last time," my heart said.
"Switch partners," Allen said.
"You did it, Leslie," my mind said.

He's a good guy whose intensity will serve him well in the right outlet. His intensity is close to what my Beast's was, minus the dirty root. That's what scares me the most.

3.22
Red Flag of a Different Color
Dear Diary,

I told Prince Charming my one requirement for a car was AC. Anything else was gravy. I don't handle heat well. It makes me sick in a myriad of ways. Partly why I don't particularly like training gi Jiu Jitsu. I would not be surprised to find out I have undiagnosed blood pressure issues due to my struggle to stay conscious during extreme heat.

He told me my transmission was going out. We sold my car. He eventually brought me home an adorable little red car. I loved it. However, he said it had no AC. It was winter and he promised to fix it by summertime.

The cold months came and went. It grew warmer and I began to remind him it needed fixed. He said we would get to it. He said were it not for the repairs his car needed done, he would have. He said there was still time. I waited.

It got hot and I began to get sick. My job in disaster restoration I had gotten in order to hide my bruises, was brutal. I had hoped my heat tolerance would strengthen. It never did. Days were spent fighting to stay conscious as my vision swam in a moving fog. I was miserable, but I loved helping people get their homes and lives back. It's the one place I felt like a hero. So, I fought the heat.

I began to beg and nag. I told him how sick I was. How I had to often puke in a garbage bag from the heat. How my social time was cut short by the need to drive the 35 minutes home to shower, only to arrive at my best friend Kat's house, drenched in sweat from the drive.

Paired with my bedwetting insecurities which still hung like outdated skeletons in my closet, I hated smelling bad from the sweat. It felt like a bitch slap. I was halfway back to my bedwetting shame.

The hot months came and went. He didn't fix it like he promised. I continued to ask/beg/nag/remind him. He said there was no need to fix it during the winter months. He said there was still time before next summer. He said if I would stop nagging him so much he would have already. He said we didn't have the money. Excuses poured from his lips. Doubt, and reality, began to claw my mind.

I didn't want to believe it, but I could see the pieces of my Beast's game. Confirmed when the next year, was rinsed and repeated. For 2 years I'd had that car. 2 years his promise remained unfulfilled. I began to question what was true.

Was he doing it on purpose? He knew how miserable I was, yet he did nothing about it. Did he want me that way? When paired with his inopportune smiles, the answer appeared ugly. I never wanted to believe he enjoyed hurting me, but the evidence was piling high.

I was confused. I thought bad guy stuff was direct, obvious, and action oriented. Beast simply wasn't doing something. Did that mean he was intentionally doing the opposite? By not fixing my AC, did that mean he was intentionally keeping me miserable? Could I blame him for something he didn't directly do but his actions were indirectly causing? See the confusion? I do. I was there.

Retrospect has since taught me this is where we women fool ourselves. We focus on what he is doing now, rather than connecting the dots from the past to see the big picture. It's in the big picture we see the patterns in his personality, not just the best in his person.

Looking at the big picture, I do believe he was doing it on purpose. I believe hide and defeat was his game. He smiled sometimes when he hurt me, and he always was one step behind, hiding in the shadows, or one step ahead, ready to stop me. That's the artistry of con-men.

It's what we are looking for, that determines everything. He was looking for someone to blame for his life. He was looking for a target. I was looking for Prince Charming. I was looking for a way out of my hometown. Someone in Jiu Jitsu might be looking for a triangle where someone else sees an armbar. It's all real. It's all there. It's what we believe, that creates our reality.

I didn't want to believe I had fallen in love with a truly bad man. But I had. I just couldn't see the reg flag, because it came disguised in a different color. Or maybe that was all the glitter I covered my life with.

3.23
Desperate Dizzy Dictionary
Dear Diary,
 I tried once to get mad at him. To build, cultivate, and explode the anger within me. But I couldn't, because it wasn't there.
 I began to yell at him, calling him every bad name I could think of, the way he had so often done to me.
 I sounded stupid. I sounded like I was reading a list of bad names from the dictionary. With no emotion to back them, they sounded mechanical. I felt fake. He found it funny, and began to laugh at me. His words spoke what was in my mind. I began to hurt.
 He started his name calling me then. My words stopped, and my tears began to flow.
 I didn't want to feel what those words meant, towards him. Regardless of their truth. So why was I then trying to cultivate it? Why was I trying to make bad? Because I was desperate and didn't know what else to do.

3.24
Growth
Dear Diary,
 I have a tingly feeling something great is going to happen today. The last few days have been exhilarating.
 "You are enough to fight for," God said.
 "I don't believe it, yet," my heart said.
 "Why not?" God asked.
 "I don't have a good reason not to," my mind admitted.
 I'm going to write a beautiful story today.
 Reviews on triangles, I finally got through the steps.
 The best part came in the free rolls. 3 minutes with Allen awarded me my first, "Nice shot!" though I'm not sure what he was referring to. I didn't get any closer to a submission with him, but it felt different. I don't know what he saw.
 Hunter, the up and coming boxer joined us for the first time in Jiu Jitsu. God gave me an opportunity to pay it forward and grow him the same way Shelby helps grow me. He and I rolled for an hour after class. I guided, and he smiled. A lot. His boxing skills helped him see the openings. Unlike my stubborn mind

which needs a ridiculous amount of repetition for something to stick to its slippery surface, I needed only to teach him once for his mind to hold on. 60 minutes changed him. His confidence arose, his smile widened, and I took another brother under my wing. I love helping people.

Today was good.

3.31
Meeting My Dragon
Dear Diary,
It happened, during a new position called the prison lock, which looks like a bad piggyback ride. One with their arms around the front of your neck, and their legs locked around your hips. I saw Miranda light up when chosen to be Allen's partner. It was beautiful.

My mind was on helping the new girls, and helping train Frank, who had signed up for his first fight.

I chose Allen for the final freeroll round.

I watched where his arms went, and dove under when I saw them raise. Without seeing the steps I took to get there, I suddenly found myself locked, and fighting a rear naked choke. We were in the prison lock.

What I can only describe as a gloved claw creeping over me, gripped my body. I froze in fear, as I felt my walls fall. The walls I had built to strengthen the dam around the pressure of my past. My body froze, my dam broke, and my mind exploded.

Suddenly I was in a tornado of feelings, memories, and questions.

Bad feelings, almost mad feelings, and sad feelings.

Lowlights of memories flashed like lightning in my mind. Long enough for a gut punching reminder, short enough for me to not find my footing and stay there, fast enough to take my breath away, and slow enough to pressure me with pain.

Questions flooded my mind in breaking waves of unanswered and unrelenting sorrow: Why me? Why did he hurt me? Why was he smiling? What did I do to do to deserve it? Why didn't I defend myself? Why was I not good enough for daddy to give me away? Why do I still piss the bed? Where is my happy ending?

I rode the waves, it was all I could do. Waves of memories, paralysis, questions, waves of uncontrollable tremors traveling through my body. Allen's lock stopped my body from convulsing. Arms around my neck, legs around my hips, I was prison locked, in ironic safety.

I'm not sure what he did, or what he knew, or what he saw. I do know time seemed to freeze for me, for an eternity. Lost in the dizzying tornado of my tumultuous past.

I think he let go. I remember the lock releasing, myself rolling over, and my mind blacking out. The next minutes of memories are strung together like a strobe light.

I should have taken a minute, but I was stubborn. "Come on, let's go," I remember saying mechanically. I remember being in mount on who, I don't know. The laps we took, the end of class questions and answers, and most of the rest of the day, is a blur.

"You will get locked in that position, where you cannot move. Leslie saw some of that today," Allen said. He was trying to pull me back to reality. I couldn't reply. My body hadn't reset yet. I could only nod.

I could barely high five him at the end of class. My body was all too slowly regaining control of itself.

"See? It wasn't that bad," he said.

It wasn't bad, but it wasn't good either. Not what I had planned or wanted.

Now I'm in bed, crying. I don't know where to go from here.

APRIL IS 11 HEAVEN

Trigger Warning
April 2nd
Dear Ladies,
Dear Leslie,
Dear Diary,

Have you ever looked back on your life, and wished you could change it? Change a moment, your direction, your mind, your choice? I have. I do. Several moments, in fact. Leading into a night that changed my life, forever, not for better, for worse.

If I could go back, I'd meet 23-year-old naive Leslie, whose innocence and ignorance, was going to force her to pay a price.

I'd start by telling her, she is worth so much more than she thinks. And she doesn't deserve what is about to happen to her.

I'd tell her, find a back corner of the bar to talk to her father figure that night. The private matters she wanted his advice on, would not be heard by anyone else. Do not bring him home. Do not go behind closed doors. 2 years of advice and talk about God, life, philosophy, and politics, is not enough time to truly know someone. People hide their ugly side when the lights are on.

I'd tell her, while she thought her martial arts training was preparing her for a nameless mugger in her Nashville streets, that's not where her attacks were going to come from. They were going to come from the men she loved.

I'd tell her love is blind by filter, not by darkness. The face in front, hides the actions behind. Love sees the face, the name, before the character traits.

I'd tell her, while it wasn't violent, it was violation. It was rape. It was rape by a coward, as he took away her ability to say no by taking her while she was sleeping.

I'd tell her to not kick herself, for yet again freezing in fear instead of enacting her martial arts training. Nothing can prepare anyone for such pain.

Pain dug deeper as the pointing fingers of the police officers, tried to poke holes in her side. "Is this worth ruining his life over?" they rinsed and repeated. She froze again. She felt the gavel saying "guilty" and it crushed her newly broken self. She didn't want to fight or defend herself anymore. She just wanted it to be over.

In her mind she did the math: one worst night for her, vs years of him in prison misery. Had she known how much life this was going to cost her for years, she might have made a better decision. She decided to bury the skeleton in her closet, and deal with it alone, bone by bone. She was so scared, backed into a corner with the weight of his life on her tired shoulders, and she cowered and caved into submission.

I'd tell her not to let her dad's words hurt her as much as they did. In his mind he was saying what he believed was right. As much as she was hoping he would finally be her hero, he just wasn't, with words that need not be told. I'd tell her to let his hurtful words, at her most hurting time, be the line she needed. Either to cut ties, or cut the thread of hope for a hero father she was so desperately clinging to. I'd tell her if she continued to hold her breath, holding out for him, she would pass out. Let go, and let it out Leslie. Stop giving him opportunity to say "No." Hope, but don't expect, Leslie. Hope leaves the door open; expectations leave a frame to fill. Expectations are holes we dig within ourselves for someone else to fill. Better just to pray for him, not wait for him.

I'd tell her, had she known what she needed to know about sex-ed, she would have faced an impossible choice. A choice she wouldn't want to make. As bad as this traumatic experience was, it was better this way.

I'd tell her to smoke weed that night, not drink. It would be better for her. She'd remember, she'd see, she'd think, she'd find a way to a happy ending. I'd tell her, drinking, to cover pain, instead of to celebrate, was a road to a dark place. But that night it changed. Alcohol went from party popper, to bandaid.

Lastly, I'd tell her trying to forgive him was going to be one of the hardest things she'd ever do, but it would be worth it. It would free her.

To all you beautiful ladies reading this book for whatever reason led you to it, here is what I will tell you. Love yourself. You are enough. You are worth more than what they took from you.

It's ok to hate him, for a while. Hold that wall, heal yourself. Then let go, but learn.

Learn the signs we women love to look for. While we are looking for the signs saying "Yes," we miss the red flags in our faces. The ones our girlfriends are telling us we don't see. We are special right? "He won't do it to me," we believe.

We are special, we are all unique, but even unique fits confined in a box, or on a target. To them, we are what they want. That's all.

Our uniqueness comes in the pathway we live life. No one can connect the dots in the same order our individual selves choose to. While we might meet on certain points, we part ways, continuing on our own barefooted road.

The trap, comes in believing because we are special, it means we don't have to do things like everyone else. Tried and true isn't true for us. We are the exception, right? I know I've said those words countless times.

Dear ladies, the fact is, sometimes we do have to do things, like everyone else. Especially the things we don't want to do. Like kicking a man's ass when he lays a hand on us. We aren't his mother. We can't save him. And yes, they do deserve it. If we don't, well, we know how that story ends too: victim or dead. We don't get to choose what life does to us, but we do get to choose what we do back to it.

Ladies, we need to fight back. We need to kick ass. We need to train in martial arts. We are smarter than we think, we know we are. Martial arts beats strength with smarts, using proper technique. I have fought 300lb+ men in the ring, and won, with my Jiu Jitsu techniques. It can be done, easier than you think.

Odds are high for women to be attacked. "It wasn't supposed to happen to me," I said time and time again, but it did. Had I known what an armbar was, I could have stopped my second sexual assault.

Think of martial arts like an insurance policy. We don't want to have to use it, but when the time comes, it's a damn good thing we bought it. Better to feel the burn in our body in training, than in our heartbreak later. There are techniques to get out from under a man pinning us. Chokes we can pull from a typical rape position. Ways to choke him unconscious within seconds when done properly. Ways to break bones and joints, with little strength needed. There are options, and doorways out.

Imagine being in a room full of women. Women who want the same thing you and I do: to become. You can insert your own personalized word goal at the end of that sentence. It's different for all of us. Imagine fighting for that goal, with a group of women wearing inspirational quotes on their tank tops, or a gi, depending on the martial arts style you choose. Imagine all the women, including you, are going in the same direction: up. Those women will become friends, family, sisters. All the while helping you climb as you do the same for them. Using each other for support, as drops of sweat, and probably a few tears, fall to the mat. Pretty picture isn't it? Wait till you see, and feel it in person. It's empowering.

I can already hear the excuses coming ahead in time. "I don't have the time." You have 24 hours in a day. "I don't have the money." Give up something of less value. "I can't, I have medical issues." As do I. I haven't let it stop me. "You're different from me." The only difference is I made a choice. A choice to say "Yes," a choice to go. Do not let words be the only thing stopping you.

The choice is yours. Pay for the security, and fun, of martial arts now, or pay for therapy later. It happened to me. It can happen to you too. It's sad, but true.

Martial arts give you the ability, knowledge, and skills, to write your own ending, as your own hero.

Are yall convinced yet? If not, keep reading. Keep reading anyway. This story has a very happy ending.

4.3

Christmas in April

Dear Diary,

Today I am cracking a bit, unsure of where.

I am crossing lines, and not good ones. Taking things, a bit too far. Risk comes cheap when you're broke and have little to lose.

I pulled from my last Jiu Jitsu class a move to get out of side control beneath heavy men. It didn't work, but something did.

I moved differently. I stayed close, slithered, and saw more openings than I ever had.

3 arm bar attempts on me later, I pulled out of each one at the last second. I found and felt a moment where their grip loosened, and I yanked. After the last one I somehow muscled through and found mount. It was cool. I grinned, he smiled, and I cheesed. Giggles bubbled from my lips. I began baiting arms bars just to see if I could get out of them.

Unfortunately, my chance to show Allen was stopped by his words: "Don't give him your arm!" he emphatically said. But it's what I wanted. Ego bruised, I tapped.

Free rolling took a side step as the boxing guys took the floor before class. I sat with sweet Frank.

"You're doing better in your training," I said. I told him where I thought his strengths and weaknesses were: very similar to my own. We both tried hard, but took too many hits before we reacted.

"You need to give it your all. Your opponent will be too. You're just trying to make yourselves better. In this ring, in ours, nobody loses." His eyes shifted. I had hit something in him.

He cleared his throat and said, "This next round, this one is for you." Tears sprung to my eyes. Frank was such a sweetheart.

"Thank you, Frank, that means so much to me."

His eyes were swimming behind shiny tears, but he was holding it together. The bell was about to ring.

With a smile on his face and newfound pep in his step, he boxed, he fought. I watched like a proud big sister. He fought his precious big heart out.

I followed the ending bell with a double high five and a "That was amazing Frank, thank you." He smiled. He was growing. It was beautiful.

My own growth came after some lengthy drills, Frank and I paired up.

First roll I was the odd woman out. The goal was to stay out of any position. I watched and learned.

Andrew, the Italian, was big and solid, I wanted a second chance with him. Mitchell was happy, having a good day from the looks of it. Chance, cheery and finding Kimuras everywhere, as always. Miranda, little spitfire, happy to have her buddy Lucas in class. Lucas, spider monkey man, kept getting his favorite position: backpack.

I tailored the way I rolled towards the body type of my partner. Stayed high away from Andrew who liked to use his body weight to slow people down. I corkscrewed away from Chance's long arms and legs. Mitchell, I matched for strength, and smiled a lot with him. Lucas, I used speed to power through his lightning fast arms and legs.

Midway through my roll with Chance, I became partially blind. A light flashed in my vision, and I lost my peripherals, seeing only through a tunnel. My body numbed over, and my right cheek and shoulder twitched. It was weird.

"Tap so it doesn't hurt tomorrow," Chance said with my arm in an armbar. I couldn't feel it, but he knew I was pushing too far.

I could control my body, but not feel it.

I matched Lucas for speed, doubling mine. We rolled faster than we ever had. 3 taps from him, and we kept going. I guess the numbness has its advantages.

The surprise came when Miranda came up to me during the cool down laps: "I really liked how you kept going. That was some intense shit." My heart swelled. I didn't know she had been watching. "Been working on my rebound time, I didn't want to stop," I replied. "It was pretty awesome," she said.

Yes, I wanted to cry happy tears.

4.4
Sexual Assault and Happy Endings
Dear Diary,

My second sexual assault, an armbar would have stopped, but I didn't know what that was.

I don't want to dive into the details, but the situation was eerily similar to my rape. Rinse and repeat at its worst.

I should have gripped, and pulled. Instead I threw, and threw him out.

"I'm sorry, I'm sorry," he muttered as he ducked out the door.

"Not again!" my heart ached.

"You fought back this time," my mind said.

As my tears fell in the shower in the following weeks, so did half of my hair.

I had long ago suspected I would be tested. Like Samson in the Bible. Was my strength and beauty in my hair or in my God? I knew I had too much pride in my hair. It was the only thing about me I felt was worth anything. The most beautiful thing about me. I thought I'd get cancer and lose it when I was old.

I got a bitch slap when I was 30.

Tears and hair fell in the shower. For weeks I cried as my hair kept falling out. I began to cuss at God again. It was just too much. Situationally too similar to my rape, and now I was losing half of my hair? What had I done to deserve this? I was almost mad at God.

Leaning against the cold walls of the shower, I once again imagined Jesus holding me.

Yes, simultaneously I was cussing into the arms that held me. Into the arms that love me.

"Thank you," God said.

"Why?!" my heart bled from my fresh wound.

"You'll see," God said.

A year later, I had my answer. But first, I have to tell you a back story.

I was born with big bouncy curls. I looked like a doll. As the years grew my hair long, the weight of it, pulled the curls straight.

I have chased curls ever since. Curling irons, sponge rollers, rag rollers, anything I could find, I tried.

I feel the most beautiful when my hair is curly.

A year after the sexual assault, I had my happy ending. I had curls. The baby hairs filling in where the old strands had fallen out, were curly. Framing my face with curls prettier than the ones I had faked.

Every day the curls are different. I never know if my curls are going to be big or little, tight or loose, or how the curl is going to curve. It feels like my own personalized sunrise on my face. I was finally thanking God, and apologizing.

Was it worth it?

Yes.

4.7

Pull Up Up and Away

Dear Diary,

I didn't know where to go, so I prayed the Lord would lead.

"Do a pull-up," He said. My goal is to be able to do one by summer, though I haven't been practicing. I depended on pushups and tire flipping to build my strength. I love tire flipping. Makes me feel like a badass.

My hands gripped the bars. I found my grip, and pulled. My chin made it over the top! Over a foot higher than my last attempt!

I did it! I did my first pull up!

Yes, I want to cry happy tears.

4.10

The Escape

Dear Diary,

My lips are smiling as the sunlight streams on my hands pecking away at this keyboard. I'm writing in my car, instead of inside the gym for the first time.

I realized I prepare for bad with too much of my time. I've had multiple conversations with Allen about how scared I am of the choke, giving fuel to a fire that has barely even started. Burning myself with a fear of something unknown, unlived, and under God's control.

The best thing to catch the bad with, is a surprise. It's going to hit either way. I've let fear dig a blackhole in me. I don't want life to go in that direction anymore. I want to go up, like a star.

The difference in dreaming, trying, working, and succeeding, is where you stop.

Allen and Prydacted are going on a much-deserved vacation. I have a chance to be alone, figure out what is inside me, without Allen guiding me. What am I truly made of, like he asked a month ago of me.

He will be gone long enough I could find out. At the end, I do want to do it alone. Just me and God. Find the fight in me, instead of the defense.

...

I'm sitting here, laptop in my lap, stars shining through the sun roof above me, 2 purple flowering trees standing like a door frame in the mulch in front of me. Tears begging to fall like happy raindrops, I'm holding them back. There are better things to do than cry. I did it.

The last time I was in a parking lot writing was nearly a decade ago. A coffee shop parking lot. My home, my awakening world, where I had a group of friends from all walks of life, all just trying to make their way there, and back home again.

Now I sit, with a better story to write. A happy ending.

The door to the ring opened multiple doors tonight: we were asked what we wanted to work on, where we find ourselves stuck. My mind ran through my rolls, and took a step back. The choke was my dragon, but the backpack opened the door to let the dragon through. One step ahead meant never opening that door in the Jiu Jitsu chess game. Position before submission, as is the saying in Jiu Jitsu. If I beat the position, the submission is beaten too.

"How to get out of backpack before it's clinched," I said. This time it was Mitchell on my back. Allen watching. I had to keep it together. I slowed my breathing, put my thinking cap on, and let my body take over. When I take my emotions away, my decisions become better. I need to get better at that.

We drilled, we questioned, we grew. Backpack defense, breaking guard, and sweeps. Real life decisions. How am I going to get through their legs? Where am I going to post? What are they going to use to stop me?

My moment came when Lucas got me in his signature backpack during free rolls. His arms sliding under my chin, behind my head, as the rear naked choke began to take shape. I fought. Slip sideways, push his bottom leg away, and slide over it. My hands shimmied for a monkey grip between his elbow and my chin. Before he could close the choke, I did it. As his arms slid up and over my ears, my smile split my face. I was out. I got away from the choke!

For the first time in my Jiu Jitsu training, I got out of a backpack and a rear naked choke. As I rolled away, rolls of laughter burst from my lips.

"I did it!" I panted.

Lucas grinned. "You've been waiting for this moment for a long time." My heart surged.

Waves of pride that I had finally escaped, relief that I now knew the way, and a level up in joy, coursed through my veins. I was giddy.

It felt like I was on Cloud 9 for the remaining rolls. Or the cloud was inside me like a morphine rush. I couldn't tell. Either way, it was heaven.

Position before submission. While I didn't avoid the backpack and rear naked, I did find and follow the path leading out.

The fire will come, someday. For now, I think I'm finding this inner peace thing. My heart is warm and swirling. Like there is a little girl dancing in my chest. Happy, twirling, and not quite sure which way is up.

4.13

Firefall

Dear Diary,

As me and a friend pulled out of the pancake house, beneath rolling gray skies, I looked down. My red hair fell like a waterfall over my gray tank. It glowed like fire.

I've been praying to God to help me find my fire for weeks now. And there it was.

"You've had it all along," God said.

My heart giggled.

"I think I'm going to end my book here," my mind said.

4.21

Plans, Break

Dear Diary,

It's Easter Sunday and I get to arise and tell Allen I finished my first book.

I walked in, and promptly clumsily dropped my gym bag, my purse, and my aloe drink. I laughed. Oh well.

"I finished it," the words broke through my grinning lips before "Hello" could. "The first book." Allen's eyes gleamed.

My lips couldn't stop grinning.

"I found my fire. Not what I expected, but it's a happy ending."

"It never ends the way we think it will."

"I'm just, I, I did it," I giggled and stammered.

With one of the biggest smiles I've seen on his face, his lips said, "Congratulations!" as his arm opened for a well-earned hug. My most proud moment yet.

"Thanks!" I giggled. My cheeks hurt from smiling so much. "The next book will start with the Jiu Jitsu camp I need to sign up and pay for.

He smiled.

I then went and did my second pull-up, just to prove to myself it wasn't a dream. Chin above the bar, I held myself up, and just enjoyed the view. Began to lower a couple inches, got really excited, and pulled myself back up. Another one. My goal was to be able to do one before summer, and I did 2.

This is one of the best days of my life.

4.22

88mph

Dear Diary,

Spoiler alert: my book didn't end there.

"It never ends the way we think it will," Allen said.

"What's next?" my heart asked.

"Keep moving," my mind said.

4.23

The Beginning

Dear Diary,

"Jiu Jitsu is all strangles and breaks," Allen said at the start of camp. My heart jumped. I never looked at it so simply. It means this battle will never end. As long as I live, I have to fight. Somehow, I forgot about that.

The moves we were taught were foundations: sweeps, shrimps, and arm drags.

"You get to decide if you are going to go in or out," Allen said as he shot a stare my way. "In, to reposition, or out, to get away." Sounds like the choice to fight, or fly.

Mitchell and I paired up, and he asked who wanted to go first. He's a good guy.

"I will." I slid into position, and out of my feelings.

He backpacked me, I took a deep breath, and let go.

I figured out I can mostly twist out of backpacks. Allen must have seen me because he then showed us the defense against my trick.

Eyes on me as he grinned, he said, "Now if they decide to twist out of it, here is what you do." Oh no he didn't! Yes, yes, he did.

I guess I'm doing something worthy of a fightback for him to show us the defense.

In free rolling with Mitchell I learned how to fight a little harder.

With Peter I learned how to push, and play high so his big and strong self wouldn't squish little me.

With Blake I learned how to have fun.

With Lucas, I learned speed, more twists, and how to successfully avoid his backpack. "Argh!!!" his voice growled in playful annoyance as I got out again. Mine giggled. I felt like I had leveled up. Our roll became even more fun after that.

The final bell rang with Miranda and I squaring up. Her and I had not rolled in weeks. Neither of us got a submission, but we held each other off better than ever. I learned I had to be tight, and sharp against her small frame. She smiled at the end. "Good job!" "You too girl!"

"Know the platform you are on well enough before moving on to the next level," Allen said.

4.24

Damn Break

Dear Diary,

"I need 4 or 5 people to start competing against Black Belts and winning. When you win in combat no one can say you are wrong. It will prove the theories I'm working on. Carl will belt you, but I'll help get you there."

My heart rose like the tide. Warm, energetic, and building. I felt pulled in.

Mitchell grinned. He felt it too.

My mind wandered to my old school where the pull of Black Belt tugged at me like a child trying to get my attention.

This was the right way to do it.

This pull nearly swept me off my feet.

"I'll be your Black Belt," I said.

He was mid-sentence (rude on my part) but slid in a "Thank you," as he continued. After he finished, I said, "I may not be the first, I know I'm a late bloomer, but I will be one." His eyes held a smile.

30 years old and I've begun training for a Black Belt in Jiu Jitsu. It's never too late. In free rolls I found a leg lock I liked, and managed to hold on for 45 seconds until the bell rang.

In a roll with Mitchell I was able to stop a roll from mount he started. He wanted side control, but I pushed through and made a circle. "Yes!" I exclaimed past my uncomfortable mouth piece. He smiled.

Small talk with big brained Chance led me to telling him I know the first half of the Declaration of Independence. As we rolled, I recited, until he got me in an armbar. All in good fun. I wanted to test my ability to separate my mind from my body, and he wanted to test my claim.

"Be patiently aggressive," Allen said. "There is a reason Jiu Jitsu is referred to as 'swimming with sharks.' Threaten with a smile, is how it's done."

I love sharks, yet they get my blood pumping faster than near anything. Fastest way to get me to jump watching a movie, fastest click for a documentary.

I love it here.

I'm wearing my lucky leggings. The neon jellyfish ones. Something always happens when I wear them. It's my costume right now. My dare pants. My jellyfish pants are also how I want to move in Jiu Jitsu. I want to be fluid.

I can't wait to see what's going to happen next.

...

I failed. We had one goal. And I failed. I had 21 minutes to get a submission from the back, per Allen's goal for us, and I didn't. I used every old and new idea I could think of. Nothing worked.

I'm on my period. I'm injured. I'm tired. And now I'm a failure.

After the final roll I lay on the ground for too long. Under the guise of catching my breath, I threw an inner temper tantrum and pity party.

Allen's feet came into view around my right shoulder. A reminder I needed to get up. His eyes knew something. I stood up, with trembling legs, and tears I couldn't hide, in my eyes. He was gauging me. I bet he saw my failure.

I walked the cool down lap with my head down. Hands on my hips, half holding myself up, half scolding myself.

I stared at the floor, so no one could see how close to cracking I was.

"Alright high five your partners," Allen said. I was doing alright until I clapped with him. The tears and truth dropped.

"I didn't get it," my quivering voice told him.

"That's ok. The point wasn't to get it, it was to understand it. To every up there is a swing."

It was enough to take off the edge.

"What was the worst thing about today?" he asked us at the end of class. I kept my mouth shut. One word and I knew I'd break. I know he was opening the door for me but I couldn't break the dam.

Stories were told of tight techniques, until Allen asked for the emotional bad. Another chance. I couldn't. I had to hold myself together.

"Don't take it to heart." He was speaking to me. I stayed silent.

As the students left and the lights were shut off, my trembling voice echoed through the empty gym.

"What did I do wrong?!"

We walked outside where people stood outside the restaurant next door. I had to keep it together. I wanted to cry at the gym for the first time.

We talked, we walked as he led us away from the crowd and into the parking lot. He must have seen I was crumbling.

"You did nothing wrong."

"I had 21 minutes to get the submission from backpack and I failed!" I exclaimed.

"But does that make you a failure?"

"Well no, but you asked us to do one thing. Just one. And I couldn't do it." The tears tipped over the edge of my lashes.

"Did you try for it?"

"Yes! That's all I went for. The whole time. I ditched every other plan and went for it." I was finally letting go and crying.

"Then you passed the test."

Dumbfounded, I asked, "Wait, what?"

"Leslie the point wasn't to get the submission, the point was to attempt. These things take time. I know I'm supposed to have some magical answer for you, but I don't. These things take time and hard work, but you did nothing wrong today."

His words tried hard to push past my stubborn head and into my heart where their meaning would be understood, but my low self-esteem foolishly fought them away.

Blubbering through tears, I vented, "It was supposed to change today! The sensation of a black belt finally sliding around my waist was my first thought this morning. Not God, not my To Do List. I had it. I even came here tonight with a game plan of leading with my hips instead of my arms. I wore my favorite neon jellyfish leggings to remind myself that's how I want to move. I flipped everything now that Black Belt was in sight. Today was supposed to be amazing. Nothing worked. I've been training backpack for a month now. And I still failed."

I couldn't stop the tears.

"They were looking for it today. It wasn't you that failed. You tried everything. It was them that stopped you. Leslie, you are the only woman in there against some big and strong men. That matters. You'll find it."

His words rang true. No one has ever believed in me that much. Especially not me.

"You need strength to get to the next level. Strength will enhance your technique. You'll get there. You need drills before you can find if you want to move like a jellyfish. Until you know where you are going you won't find how you want to get there."

"Will you listen to him Leslie?!" my heart begged.

"You're going to be ok," Allen said.

"Ironic how it's what you think you did to yourself, not what someone did to you, that finally made you cry," my mind pointed.

4.28

Inverted Empty

Dear Diary,

    Retrospect says that I should have outsmarted the guys' moves to get the backpack. I chose to pummel what was in front of me, instead of going around it, as I so often stubbornly do.

    A dangerous idea has been ping ponging in my mind the last few days. Wasn't sure if I wanted it to plant it or not, but here it is. I saw a saying that said, "You must always be willing to truly consider evidence that contradicts your beliefs, and admit the possibility that you may be wrong. Intelligence isn't knowing everything. It's the ability to challenge everything you know."

    I know God is real, I know the Bible is true, I just do. But what if it's not? What am I left with? Me. Just me. Who am I?

    I know I've used the Bible and God to lead, justify, and create value for my seemingly useless life. I've based my life around Him, and have lost and forgotten myself.

    If I am wrong about God, what, within me, is worth anything? I don't know.

4.29

The Point

Dear Diary,

    Jiu Jitsu camp is turning into Jiu Jitsu bootcamp. The only thing that stopped me from joining the military was knowing my body is too broken to physically handle it. I'm weak and I know it.

    I now have a fractured rib. T10, here at the beginning of Jiu Jitsu camp. Some of the worst pain of my life, but it's not stopping me.

    This next month I'm pushing my physical limits.

    At least I have an idea of where to go.

12 MAY BE A LUCKY NUMBER

May 6th
Full Circle
Dear Diary,
    One year ago, today, Beast pulled his con artist phone trick.
    Today, I wrote a children's book, per Allen's challenge. Wrote and partially sketched.
    "Hear me ROAR!" boomed my heart.
    "Finish it," Allen said.
    "Don't stop," my mind pushed.
    Walking into the gym with my sketchbook, I smiled.
    I grinned when Allen looked my way. I handed him the book, "I did it!" He looked intently. His hands flipped through the pages like a whip.
    I watched his face ride the train of my story. A smile here, a stare there, an understanding, running through.
    "You're dead set in the right direction. Keep the momentum, and don't stop till you reach the end." His voice took on a stronger tone. He was pushing me.
    "Go!" he said, his hands shooing me out the door.
    I giggled and said I was savoring the moment.
    "That's good, but don't stay there. Go!"
    Clap went my notepad. Jingle jingle jingle went my keys.
    When I walked into the dark night of the outside, I only had 2 things on my mind, who I wanted to get the first copy of my book, 2 and what my autograph should be.
    "Just "L," so they can fill the rest in with love," God said.

5.10

Clear Truth

Dear Diary,

Even when the truth is in front of them, some will still turn away. I learned that today. It came from a friend near and dear to my heart. He didn't see the magic, only the material.

I read him my fairytale. He saw only what was wrong, not what was right. Turned me off, and turned the radio up.

I knew it would happen, but I didn't know how bad it would hurt.

I guess this is how Jesus feels, when we turn away from truth.

I can see clearly now.

5.11

A Forehead Kiss within a Daydream

Dear Diary,

One of my favorite days. A medieval festival. Costume, a turkey leg, and eye candy for the whole day. I smoked a bowl, and went alone.

I met a lady glassblower with whom I shared my story. She told me her own story of domestic violence. "If you aren't strong enough, find an equalizer, and fight," she told me. I'm never going to forget that.

I saw a silver ring, a thin silver wire tied with the tip pulled down making a heart, out of the knot. It was beautiful, I bought it. It wasn't until later God reminded me it looked like the infinity promise ring my Prince had gotten me.

God knows I love replacing memories. If the last time I went somewhere, went bad, I went back, and lived a better life story. I've had to replace a lot of drunk memories over the years. Replacing the ring was sweet. This is how He loves me.

Then God wrote a happy ending, I couldn't have dreamed.

I finally went home with a hottie from the circuit. Been wanting to for years. Bucket List. It wasn't everything I had dreamed, it was better, because of the unexpected level he took it to.

"I don't want this night to end," I said.

"Then don't. Stay over and cuddle."

"I have a dirty little secret." His arms tightened around me. I was encouraged.

"I still wet the bed," I said boldly. "Doctors can't figure out why," I said defensively.

A tear flowed out, and he caught it. My heart melted a little.

I had expected rejection, as I had experienced the few times prior, I had dared try to tell in recent years. My heart pounded as I waited for his words.

"Thank you for telling me. There is a store around the corner." My jaw dropped.

No disgust, no judgement, no pointed finger.

He thanked me. He gave me a solution. He wanted me.

"This is too good to be true," my heart fought.

"It's workable," he said.

"Isn't this what you want Leslie? Start believing in the happy," my mind mothered.

Insecurity running deep enough to pull the rug from under me, I fell back into my old habits. Instead of feeling the happy, hearing the words I'd yearned to hear, and following in the new direction my life had just taken, I fought myself. For 20 minutes I battled. Arguing with myself over a problem that existed only within me. He sat, listened, and to every "I can't" he had a way I could. I am my own worst enemy sometimes.

Finally, I said yes.

"I want to be brave. I'm tired of this costing me so much. I have to do this. Coffee, diapers, and mascara, is what I need." He smiled.

"It will be ok, whether you are wet or dry, I'll still be here in the morning."

How long had I waited to hear those words?

I came back with diapers, mascara, a grapefruit energy drink, cheese sticks, food for work, and strawberries.

I got dressed, under black pants to hide the diaper, and fought my fears. I snuggled onto his warm chest, nearly hiding.

"I probably won't sleep. It's safer to keep myself awake so I don't wet or leak."

He laughed. He freaking laughed.

"The sheets are washable." His words kept pouring kindness into the depths of my insecurity. I had never felt anything like it.

"I'm here to help. I believe in you. I believe you can sleep soundly in my arms. Whatever happens, I'll be here in the morning." Whatever the opposite of heartbreak and ache is, I was feeling it then.

His hand brushed away my fears, and the tears streaming down my cheeks.

The next morning, I awoke dry.

"You slept," he grinned.

"How do you know?"

"You snored on my chest, then I kissed you on the forehead."

Slightly embarrassed, I still couldn't help but grin.

"I did it, I really did it."

My heart smiled, the whole day.

My life had changed. So had I.

5.12

Inside and Out

Dear Diary,

Miranda stood there; arms wrapped tightly around Allen. She wouldn't let go. She was smiling.

I have always wanted an older brother. I never wanted to be the strong one. I'm only tough because I have to be.

God said, "Leslie, you don't need a hug from Allen, you need a post." He was right. Hugs are the one place I can fully let go within. But that's not what I'm here for.

I'd imagined more cushion from Allen on this barefooted road. More coddling, more gentleness.

Instead he has led me, without holding my hand. His hand merely points the way. The cushion is in the security I have in knowing he knows what he is doing. He is my hero, but only God can save me. Allen's words are challenging and truthful. In the end it's up to me to believe, and do.

I feel like a canvas he is stretching to fit and frame. It hurts but I know it will be worth it. Kind of already is, to be honest.

If I were his woman, like Prydacted is, things would be different. It would be his role to be the strong one. To hold, care, and comfort me. But he is my hero, it's his job to help me find everything I need and want within myself. Eventually I will go my own way alone. That's how this story goes.

5.13

A Mind Made

Dear Diary,

Getting out of side control was my goal for the day yesterday. Plans to pick the lightest partner were changed when Miranda chose Lucas. Peter, the big beast of a man, chose me. He must have remembered when I said I wanted to test all side control escapes against his strength. First time in my life it feels like I've been chosen for dodgeball.

"Plan your game!" Allen said. We all rolled hard. I planned my attacks based on the other person's body. I needed to stay above him so he wouldn't squish me like a bug. I stood up.

"Your hand is shaking," Peter noticed it first.

My mind ran like a girl down the hallway of options and perspectives of what was happening. From victim to fighter and everything in between.

"It's medical shit." It didn't matter to me at that moment. We rolled.

Grinning, Chance said before our roll, "I'm going to kill you!" I grinned back. "I'll just respawn."

I tapped with 11 seconds to go.

I did better at transitions but needed to stop waiting for the opportune moment.

As we high fived out Allen told me to go faster and stop doubting myself.

It's coming together. I'm, coming together.

5.15

High Prize, High Price

Dear Diary,

I immediately went for pull ups, 3 slow, in a row, non-jumping cheating ones. I did it.

Today's goal was to dominate position. I let that go as Allen told us to pick our favorite submissions, and start mapping our game.

My broken rib hurts today. I'm pushing through the pain so hard my surroundings faded to foggy white. I only saw bold colors and shapes for a while. I prayed. I needed help.

I went into the last round with the big Italian, Andrew.

"You ok?" he asked, nodding towards my back brace.

"Yeah, it just hurts today."

In the last few seconds I found my armbar from mount to attempted backpack as Andrew continued to roll. He blocked my back attempt. I spotted technical mount, from there I saw S mount, grabbed his arm, and swung my legs around. Tap! The longest sequence of moves I had done yet!

"That's perfect!" said Carl Finley, the morning Jiu Jitsu coach and one of the strongest and sweetest men I've ever met.

"Nice job!" a grinning Andrew said.

I was so proud. It was the easiest and most fluid sequence and submission I had done yet.

Clap outs came with a "Not bad!" from Allen. And a quick hug. It was all worth it.

A long talk with Carl as I told him about my book dreams, finished off the night. He asked if denial was a part of my nightmare.

"Not for me. I saw the truth, but I believed more in the happy ending I thought I could create, than what was right in front of me."

5.16
The Open Door
Dear Diary,

There it was, in blue, orange, and green: Good Fight: Gatlinburg Invitational. A Jiu Jitsu tournament.

I stared at the white page on the shiny surface of the glass desk. My heart started to race.

"Could I?" my heart wondered.

Silence, in the gym.

"It's up to you to decide," my mind mothered.

I stared at the page. An open invitation. An open door to something brave. My choice, to fight. Fight for a happy reason.

"I'm not ready. I've only been training a few months," my heart argued.

Silence, in the gym.

"You'll never be ready Leslie. You just have to do the best you can, with what you have," my mind reasoned.

I said yes. I got Godbumps.

5.19
Characters
Dear Diary,

3 new guys in class. I decided against telling them about my rib.

"Never tell anyone your weakness," they say.

Singled out for training for my first tournament, Allen began to give me instructions. "Start standing up."

A tall surfer looking dude who had strength, but little technique, was my match. "Don't hurt me," he said. I got 1 Americano and my second triangle in 3 minutes.

Last up was a skinny guy who was military. I could tell by the way he rolled. He knew some things and was eager to teach me.

The best part of the day came with Lucas. Allen watched nearby with his best in-house boxer Josh. We rolled, and I began to learn. I watched his movements, made the same mistakes twice instead of 3 times. Found a sweep and mount. I swept, followed through, and mounted.

Lucas grinned. "I'm not going easy on you anymore."

"Good, that means I'm doing something right."

"You're grappling is off the charts," Lucas said. The best in class just gave me a compliment. My heart soared.

After an evenly matched roll with Mitchell in which there were no submissions, but there was a fair fight, Allen gave us quite a compliment.

"You two are becoming dangerous." We smiled.

I am so happy.

5.21

Unnamed Demon

Dear Diary,

"Position before submission," Allen's voice echoed in my head before rolls.

The guy was quick, with arms and legs of steel. I slithered around him. Cliched. Fed him openings he took. I grabbed an easy Americano. Submissions weren't a priority, but it was there. I had to take it.

"Don't just cast spells, Leslie. Make your arm movements have a purpose." I laughed. "Your moves are about 75% of the way there. Which tells me you see it, but you are skipping steps. Context and drills will fix that."

I pushed, I panted. "You ok?" Peter asked. "Yeah, my rib is hurting today." His vibe shifted as he softened. "Ok then let's take it down a bit," he offered kindly. We slowed, I studied. Still no tap, and for some reason, I can barely remember the roll.

"Way to attack," Allen said. I had no idea what he meant.

5.22

Tattletale Body

Dear Diary,

My head is in a weird place today. Foggy from Monday's fever. A bit sad from period hormones. I don't know what I need.

Flashbacks have played across my mind in class lately. Chokes are getting to me again. It just won't stop.

I'm sad.

Shelby walked in the door. Hadn't seen him in a while. He taught, I faltered, I tried.

Instead of feeling proud of the progress I had made since he and I last rolled, I couldn't seem to find anything.

Second row Baptist second guessed everything.

What was wrong with me?

With Mitchell I found no taps. Learned only that my movements needed to be pointy to get in, as he moves in circles.

Allen was last. "Are we training?" he asked.

"Yes." I studied him, trying to make a plan of attack. He stopped everything I tried to do. The only thing I found was a new way in every time. But he would catch and trap me as soon as I got past his knees.

What is wrong with me?

Shelby knew. Shelby knew something was wrong with me in the way I rolled. Somehow, he could see it. I forgot I hadn't told him about my rib.

"Leslie every move you made protected your right side. You were on defense the whole time. You ran away. Within our first roll I had it figured out."

I hung my head. I was hurting and it was showing in ways I didn't see. Which I didn't like. I don't like my body doing things I don't know about.

"You don't know how to take care of yourself, or you do and you just won't. You see the rib as a hurdle, when you should just find a way around it."

"I can push through the pain. I'll be fine."

"Leslie, you're not only injured, you're hurt. And you're defending yourself at all costs. And it's costing you. You're smarter than this. Be smarter. Heal, and learn what you can on the side."

I listened, as my feet shifted on the floor. With each line I heard truth within his words. Words others had spoken to me many times. Frustrated at myself, tears began to spill over.

"I love that you cry," he said. "It shows that you're human. You need to take care of yourself. You'll only hurt yourself more if you hit it head on. Now I know you're a lot like me so you'll take bits and pieces of my advice and do what you want, but Leslie, you need to slow down before it costs you things you can never get back."

"Think, think, think," my heart said.

"I know it's in you," Shelby said.

"I got it!" my mind lit up.

"I need to train mount in free rolls," I said.

He grinned. "There's the Leslie I know."

5.23

Blurs and Confusion

Dear Diary,

I ugly cried in the shower today. I am so frustrated with myself. Sometimes I need to let it out before I do what I need to do. Tears blur my vision. And yes, I imagined the cold tile as Jesus' arms. I always do when I cry there.

After the tears and steam cleared, I made my Jiu Jitsu plan. A takedown. It went up in smoke when Allen sat down.

"You messed up my plan dude!"

"I know," he said grinning. Just what exactly did he know? Didn't matter now. I had to find a way past his knees of steel.

I found a way in, got swept and got hurt. My rib threw a fit. "Take a minute," Allen said. Trembling, I nodded. Round 2 was better.

I went sideways, and kept my feet away. I finally got side control on him. Seconds away from an Americano, but those knees of steel blocked me.

I got closer to taps on Allen than ever before.

"Nice shot!" he said at the end.

"What are you good and bad at?" Allen asked us at the end of class.

"I'm good at holding positions but I still take too long to decide what I'm going to do," I said.

"The longer you wait, the more time they have to plan."

I need to move faster. No, slower cause I'm injured. I don't even know.

5.29

Fear and Truth

Dear Diary,

Today I have fought to stay conscious. Pressure on the back of my skull has me spinning. It's been building for several days. My rib is stinging. My whole body tingles. Parts are going numb. I need to rest, and let doctors figure out what's wrong. I can't fight it much longer. My body wants to stop. I fight to stay conscious far too often.

My chiropractor did some amazing head clearing things for me. Brought me halfway back. Still foggy and tingling. I just want to sleep.

Been running into things today. Off balance and I have little depth perception.

I want to fall apart, and know someone will catch me.

Andrew told me to slow down. Chance told me he doesn't want to see me for 10 days after my tournament. He does want to know I'm resting.

Tyler, the coach of my circuit training class, rolled with us today. He's military, and military style scares me. The blast, the kinetic force they use, triggers me. I don't know why.

"Something about you scares me."

"Why? I'm not going to hurt you."

"I know, I'm trying to figure it out. That's why I picked you as my partner. I have to face it."

We rolled, and I didn't find my answer. Only more fear.

I did find truth in the talk Allen and I had after class:

"Fear is only conquered by accepting what is there."

"Anger is rooted in violation: You broke my rules. It's my turn to move."

"Frustration is anger that doesn't do anything."

"Your words will change when your mind does."

Allen said I don't love my Beast. Not anymore. "Love is self-sacrifice. If you're not willing to take a bullet for him, you don't love him. You need to not give a shit about him, just like he doesn't give a shit about you."

"You need a new purpose. Your Beast is the reason you started. He's not the reason for you to get better. He's not at the finish line."

I wish I knew what was.

5.31

Fairytale Days

Dear Diary,

Once Upon a Time, I was a kid at the Missouri zoo, where I met a zebra. It liked me. Must have liked the black and white striped outfit I had on. We had a moment, several actually. It started, I smiled. I called, it stepped. Close but not too close. People watched. It felt like magic.

In my young mind, the magic of that day, blended with the Bible verses about the faith of a mustard seed, movable mountains, and with God all things are possible, resulted in a fairytale that felt doable. I believed I could talk to animals, just like my fairytale Princesses. My mustard seed, was planted.

Ever since that day, I've tried to recreate that moment with stares and prayer.

I'd stare into the eyes of the animals I'd meet, and say the same wordless prayer: "The same God made both of us."

Some animals stared, some made their sounds, some ran. I kept trying, all these years, because I believe.

Faith of a mustard seed is all we need. Today, it was enough.

I was working on a jobsite, when an emerald green bird flew into the house, I was working in. It frantically beat its wings against the bedroom window pane. The men I was working with, didn't know what to do. I had a dream, and a plan.

"The same God made both of us," I wordlessly spoke. The bird stopped beating its wings against the glass, immediately.

"I'm here to help," I continued. I slowly stepped close. A breath away, it eyed me.

With a gloved hand I gathered its wings in, hugged my fingers around its tiny body, and picked it up off the window sill. It was still.

I could feel its heart beating, but it didn't fight or fly. Just eyed me.

Mine was beating fast. I nearly trembled with excitement. My fairytale was finally happening.

Slowly I walked outside. I sat on the porch steps beneath the shade of a giant tree.

Fingers still holding it, I caressed its smooth head. Its heart rate began to slow down. Mine sped up.

Tears began to blur my eyes. I took out my phone camera, and captured the moment clearly.

I loosened my grip, because love lets go. It stayed. My heart melted.

It lay in my palm, claws holding on to my glove, because it wanted to stay.

It had finally happened. I had moved a mountain with the faith of a mustard seed.

I felt like a fairytale Princess. 22 years of secretly talking to animals had rewarded me with this.

"This is love," my heart sighed.
"I'm not done yet," God said.
"This is a miracle," my mind smiled.

I can't tell you who, as they have a rep to protect. But I can tell you that same day, someone noticed my rib pain. They became my fairy godfather. A trip to the store, and they bought me what I wanted: a date with myself. Flowers, steak, Caesar salad, and wine, was my usual. What was once a monthly routine, lack of money had stopped me from lately. I'd eat, drink, and pray, all while relaxing in a bubble bath. My date night with myself and God. I usually cried happy tears. I did that night.

1 day, 2 happy endings, 1 happy Leslie, lots of happy tears.

13 REASONS JUNE CAN

June 1st

Ugly Wrapping Paper

Dear Diary,

If I didn't believe in God, I would believe this life is bullshit. It's all packaging without Him.

I am 30 years old, with little physical worth to show. It's all the invisible stuff, where my treasure is.

All the best things in life we can't actually see: love, truth, honor, joy, peace, on and on the list goes. We can see the packaging actions they produce, but we can't hold those things in our hands.

That's partly why I believe in the Bible. I can find no other rhyme or reason for everything.

Sometimes I imagine heaven as this place where we all lived before we were humans. Flying, dancing with Jesus, and living in love.

Maybe we got to choose, up there, when we were ready to come down to earth.

When we were ready for our test. A test to see if we really did know God. If we could see Him through this bullshit packaging. Like a treasure hunt.

Maybe to get here, to earth, we had to bite into a fruit from the Tree of Knowledge of Good and Evil, just like Adam and Eve. That way we would know too. History repeats itself, right?

I believe, in Genesis 3, where they covered themselves because they realized they were naked, means less about skin, and more about difference.

Their eyes had just been opened to good and evil. Difference. I believe Adam and Eve covered themselves because they saw the places on their bodies that were different from each other. They, like most of us, didn't see the beauty through the bullshit.

6.2

Boom Bomb

Dear Diary,

"We can't just work defense against side control, I have to give you a submission. Rear naked choke."

"No! He knows about my flashbacks lately. I don't want this now," my heart whined.

"You've done this before. Make it better than last time," Allen said.

"Round 2, what are you going to do?" my mind asked.

I was suddenly back in my first day in the ring hearing those words for the first time.

Another test, another choice, but this time I knew a lot more.

Fear rolled around in my body. Fear from an unknown source. I should have expected this from Allen. This is why he is my hero. He is helping me. I had to help myself by making a better decision in round 2.

I took a deep breath.

I took the position before I got put in it. Head on, is sometimes best from behind.

I took my turn. Fear and my heart still pounding. I wanted to cry. I stared at the flag on the wall.

As Miranda's arms slid around my neck, God said, "Same gift, different package."

I swallowed, accepting the fact soon I would not be able to breathe, but I'd breathe again, and be better off for the lesson learned.

I did it. A few times. One for one. Allen came to check on us the last round. Then it was over. A trickle of fear was all I had left. I smiled. We began to roll.

I had a tap on Mitchell within 10 seconds. A sweep to mount to an Americano. I laughed. Chance got me in a beautiful double armbar.

I tapped everyone but Allen, but I did get new positions and closer to submissions. Best roll yet. "Good shot!" he confirmed.

Joy unspeakable.

Despite having the best day in rolls yet, the tournament still has a question mark on the end. My rib probably won't be healed by that point.

"There is no such thing as powering through an injury," Allen said. "I'd drill, but take 2 weeks off of rolling. Rolling is what keeps re-injuring you. You're going to do what you want, but I'd let it heal."

"Thank you. I'll keep that in mind. I have something for you." I held out a red handled sword I had been given. It wasn't me, it wasn't my color.

"No man," he said smiling and shaking his head.

"Take it, I got it for you. It's your color." A giant smile on his face, he took the sword.

"I'm sorry it's not real or better quality."

"It's real enough. Reminds me of my first one."

I smiled. "Take it out, swing it around."

"Oh I will, I will. Thank you."

Full circle. My first day walking in, he was teaching a girl sword fighting. Now I was giving him one in return as a thank you.

6.5

The Letting Go

Dear Diary,

Life is what you make of it. I'm afraid I'll make a mistake.

I came in, and I made a move. Stood at the head of the mat, by the window. I changed my perspective. In hopes that one of the girls or women leaving the sushi restaurant next door, would see me. See me, a little woman, fighting big dudes, and be inspired. Inspired to believe they could too. Spoiler alert: it happened.

Several months later I was rolling with Peter, a barrel chested, happy faced, ultra-strong man who looked like he knew more than he was telling you. Proved true when he told me his former roommate is the brother of a former president. Anyway, one day, he and I were drilling and rolling in class. I looked up to see a 14-year-old girl watching us through the glass. Her eyes held curiosity, interest, and wonder. It had finally happened. I hope I inspired her. That's all I want.

I closed my eyes for rolls. I felt things. I found things.

My breathing became steady and strong.

"Find your next partner," Allen's voice said.

New guy, second roll with him, concerned and caring, he told me to do whatever I wanted to him. I rinsed and repeated mount to side control to Americano. Then I reversed it, back to mount, baiting him with a way out, taking technical mount, and going for an armbar. I grinned.

The dots are connecting.

While Allen gave a talk to the beginners in the class, Lucas and I kept going. Eyes closed, he swung for backpacks again and again. No. Not today. I do not want to be choked. I remembered to get rid of the leg. 3 times I got out, grinning, and near giggling. Beating the position before the submission.

"Yes!" I panted. He grinned.

Claps and bow out. I am believably happy.

6.9

Deja Who?

Dear Diary

God, the Universe, Energy, Life, a matrix, whatever you call it, when you finally fight for something, will always challenge you.

With Allen and Shelby's help, I'm beginning to see it. How they know what they know, I don't know.

Second to Allen, Shelby sees what's really going on. Detroit street smarts. He knows how to cut through the bullshit, but he's Southern Mama raised. He gets a hall pass for a Yankee converted southerner.

I'm nervous in front of him too. Like he's raising a score card I know is true. He called the rib right.

I caught myself clinging, when I should have been pushing. Caught in a position in rolls with Allen, I realized my hand was pulling his leg to me, when it was better to post against it. I changed it.

Second roll with Allen, I finally figured out one of his tricks.

"You don't go into guard!"

He laughed, "No, I ain't that stupid!" I grinned.

Shelby was last. I couldn't get anything on him. My plan, belly flopped. Within the last few seconds, my rib spasmed. Shelby stopped. He knew.

"Woah, you ok?"

I wasn't.

We sat, I rested, we talked. Somehow, we the words, 'Detroit street smarts' got said, and I had a rinse and repeat deja vu moment. I showed him the paragraph I had written before class, containing those words. I watched as his jaw dropped as he read my words.

"Shelby, you in this deep."

6.14

Empty Bed, Empty Nest

Dear Diary,

In 2 weeks, it will be 2 years since he left. I've still not filled the imprint he left behind.

The bed is still too empty.

Pillows aren't as soft as skin. They don't hug you as tight as arms do either. Teddy bear arms are too small.

Unfolded laundry piles on the bed don't have a heartbeat.

I got drunk tonight, because I'm sad.

I got kicked out of a particular area of life today. It cost me one of my most treasured possessions. I'm learning not to give people things that could be used for leverage. This is the last time I give that person any part of me I can't afford to lose. I'm learning to build walls and boundaries. I'm tired of believing the best, paying the price, of my own naivete. I'm living and I'm learning.

Life hurts right now.

6.15

Ideas

Dear Diary,

On July 4th it will be 2 years since our unhappy ending. Only July 4th I asked for an hour of Allen's time. On July 4th I need something to break, or a wall built.

"Ah, you're talking physiologically," he replied.

"Yes, and you decide where. I just need a firework that day."

Tomorrow I may ask for a choke to blackout. I need to take it one step further. Knowing when I wake up, I'll be ok.

"Sounds kind of crazy to me," my heart said.

Silence.

"Head on, is not a good idea," my mind agreed.

"I should pull out of the tournament. I'm too hurt," my heart conceded.

"Might not be a bad idea," my mind agreed.

"You need to get aggressive, like a jungle cat. Get on top, and stay on top. That's your goal for the next 2 weeks while training," Allen said.

"11 seconds, make something happen," Allen said in my first roll.

I took a breath, and flung his legs one way, my body the other, and dove in past his guard, on the outside. He fought me hard with his knees but I managed to twist in sideways, and take side control. I did it!

My heart smiled.

"Step by step," my mind guided.

"Again," Allen said.

6.17

Sprawl

Dear Diary,

"You're going to have to do the one thing that scares you the most: attack," Allen said.

"You're using your beliefs as an excuse not to do what you need to do. You were taught to be quiet, be a submissive housewife, and never fight. Your beliefs should empower you, not hinder."

Tears filled my eyes as truth filled my heart.

"You believe anger is bad. Anger is just an emotion. Mad, is active anger. It's there people do wrong. You have every right to be angry about what happened to you. Now what are you going to do with it? Are you going to attack or not? If not, Jiu Jitsu may not be for you. Maybe kickboxing is."

My heart stirred. Defiant, a touch of rebellion, I don't like being told I can't do something. I do like proving people wrong, especially about me.

"My fight isn't in kickboxing. That's not how he did it. Jiu Jitsu is, mostly. Anyway, what do I need to drill for the tournament?"

"Sprawls, start there. You probably won't sweep so you need to get to back from a sprawl."

I took the tire I loved flipping so much, and drilled sprawls until my rib told me to stop.

My military friend asked to roll. I grinned. Time to put the reps into practice.

I stanced, I sprawled, I did everything Allen said. I got and kept top mount, when lost and put into guard I used my sweep, it worked, and I gained side control. When he got in my guard, I shrimped and stood to get back on top. I broke backpack early by seeing and catching his leg. It was working.

"Tomorrow you're going to sprawl on the floor. Wednesday you're going to choke everyone out, or I'm throwing you to the gauntlet."

"What does that mean?"

"It means you will sit in the middle of the ring, while everyone else attacks you, one by one, until you tap. No breaks, no rest."

My fear must have shown on my face.

"Why are you afraid Leslie?" Allen asked. "Nothing bad has happened. You came here with the goal of never feeling powerless again. Never being put in those positions again. If you want that goal, you have to attack."

I now sit, rain pelting on my car as I write out the day, as I always do.

I want to believe. I believe in God so much. I want to believe in myself too.

6.18

Making Good Choices

Dear Diary,

I just made my first pitch. I emailed the tournament asking if I could speak at it.

Is it just me or is the sun shining a little brighter today?

"Those that want it, don't talk, they do," Allen said. Laughing, I said, "I understand," and walked away to train. He didn't know about my email.

Sprawls on the body bag. Over and over. Stood it up, let it fall, and timed myself. Over an hour.

Drilled head and arm triangle next. Over and over, moving fast enough I wouldn't have time to criticize myself. Just find and feel the move.

I am doing it.

6.19

Up and Down

Dear Diary,

Free rolls began. I choked. All my drills before class were replaced by "Choke everyone out, or I'm throwing you to the gauntlet."

Allen was first. My voice wavered as I said, "I'm not ready."

Unsure of how to attack, I fed and hooked until something happened. The roll is a blur of a memory. I know I pushed hard, tried a guillotine, and felt like I sucked.

The rest of the rolls blurred into a tornado where little was salvageable.

I remembered to choke, barely. 44 seconds on the clock left me little time to get into a position to at least try with my last partner. I don't remember how I did it, but I did.

I want to tell you what I did wrong, but that would beat the purpose. It doesn't matter anyway. Yes, I'm trying to convince myself too. Changing my own mind is hard, but I want to.

"Good roll," Allen said. I wonder what he saw.

6.21

The Yes Fight

Dear Diary,

"I need to see you God, I need to feel You," my heart and voice cried last night.

"Look at your email Leslie," God said. I found Him.

***

"Hi Leslie...or shall I say, CHAMPION 'dragon slayer',

Welcome to the Good Fight.

And you don't have to thank ME... thank yourself for being brave enough to STEP UP and fight...atta' girl!

And GOOD FOR YOU...go ahead and write your next chapter at the Good Fight. Our entire staff will be rooting for you.

It sounds like fear, battering and demons are your PAST...and your FUTURE is empowerment, faith, facing giants and reaching your finish line!

So, what are you waiting for...your ignition of inspiration has begun! GO after it.

Inspire on,

Jimmy.

P.S. We can't give you mic at the tournament...but if you have flyers or info about your cause we don't have a problem with you putting that stuff out on a table or something. I've attached Sheryl onto this email. She is in charge of admin and can help you from here if you want to put any info out.

P.P.S. Now go knock out a 'giant'...in your path to amazing!"

***

"Remember, you are fighting for Me, not against something. Attack to drive, not destroy. Love wins," God said.

"Wow!" my heart said.

"Wow!" I said.

"Wow!" my mind said.

6.22

Belief

Dear Diary,

It's stirring. The cauldron I let sadness simmer in for so long, is brewing something sweet.

4 hours of training alone today and my takeaways are great:

I need breaks for all 7 positions. From there I need an attack for each one. A two-step. A dance. I drilled. Learned a guard break, pass, to a side control I found. From side control I found the kimura.

From there I reviewed what I knew.

"You need to attack Leslie. It's time. You're ready." Sweet stirrings from God. I stopped arguing.

I learned and drilled a takedown. From the takedown I found a pass. From the pass I found mount. Mount to Americano. I did it.

I smiled. I wanted to cry happy tears.

2 hours left.

Breaking positions, side control was next. I found a way out. 3, actually.

By the end, I had new pieces, new sequences, and finally, the beginnings of belief.

Tomorrow I will attack, as soon as we clap in, I'm going for a takedown.

The smile will come out tomorrow.

6.23

Living and Learning

Dear Diary,

I wish I could say I did it, but I can't, but it wasn't for lack of trying.

I want to cry it out. Those feelings are in the way. I learned a lot. That's what I'm going to tell you about.

"It's not a dragon to slay, it's a match and it's your partner," Allen said. My mindset was flipped from the start.

My best friend Danyce came to roll. Finally got to train with a woman.

Through the class I learned drills are harder to spot in rolls than I thought. I saw some in the last quarter of rolling, Finally.

Also learned my grunts of pain are a verbal tap out. Referee doesn't want the partners to get hurt.

Tomorrow I may put duct tape on my mouth. I can't make noises then.

Today my problem was follow through, especially on takedowns. They scare me.

I saw stars a few times. Laid on the floor for arguably too long. Allen helped me up.

I don't know where to go from here.

6.24

Feel the Happy Leslie

Dear Diary

I have to eat my own words. I found 295 likes and 44 comments on a mini story from this book I posted in a sisterhood group on Facebook today. My words are working to inspire, just like I've always dreamed. I am getting there.

I got mad at myself today, and took it out on Cody during an aggressively sloppy roll. I apologized later.

Carl showed us how to pull guard off a standing grip. Half guard, sweep and mount. I liked it. Got to train it with Danyce in class today. Maybe it's better than a head on takedown.

Maybe I don't have to do what scares me the most. Why force something when it's not being called for?

"I think I've heard this before," my heart said.

Allen has said it.

"You have, 100 times!" my mind said.

6.24

I Said Yes

Dear Diary,

Godbumps tickled my skin as I walked the concrete runway to the dress shop next door to the gym. My hand gripped the cold steel handle.

A cold blast of magical air met me at the door. I'd seen this before.

Teal blue walls, circular racks of white dresses, dark blue panels covering dressing rooms, the tap of my ballet flats on the floor. I'd been here, in my dreams.

It wasn't Deja Vu. It was a dream. A month prior I'd had a dream where I'd seen this. This is where I'm supposed to be. Felt like my feet were walking into a glass slipper.

Within minutes I was telling the shopkeeper my story. Her eyes took on their own sparkle as I spoke.

As the story ended, my feet began walking. My fingers began touching the silks, satins, chiffons, and sparkles. Soaking in the real-life fairytale before my eyes.

Through the sparkly forest in all colors imaginable, I wandered.

This story is a bit private. Just me and God.

I wandered. I admired. I dreamed. I saw. I was happy.

6.25

Balance

Dear Diary.

I walked into the gym with an idea. Medicine ball.

For the next 3.5 hours, I rolled on the ball.

Time slowed down as my music played on. I had 3.5 hours to play, to find things.

I must have fallen 100 times as I practiced my positions on the ball. It moved, like a human could. I had to fight to get my balance back.

My left arm seized. I fought it, I held it, and I moved on. Enough of that story.

I began to find positions within the balance. I found mount first. Squeezed hard. I'll have a thigh gap within no time. Side control, half guard, a bit of on my back my rib fussed at me for, S mount, and transitions. I found it all.

I held each position as long as I could, and moved on.

"Learn to fall, Leslie," God spoke. From mount to a superman, I didn't waste time thinking. I just flowed. Felt where I needed to counterbalance.

My rib popped as I rolled. A bit of pain, a lot of pressure. Uhoh. X Rays tomorrow to make sure I'm ok.

I wasn't sure what I wanted to find at the finish line, but I was enjoying getting there.

As the clock struck 9pm, I found myself in mount on the ball. Comfortable, relaxed, and happy with what I'd gained.

I did it.

That's enough

6.26

Broken Body

Dear Diary,

My body broke tonight. 3 days before my tournament. Rhabdomyolysis, Allen called it. Hell, I call it.

I trained for my tournament for 8 hours today. Drilled my takedown to position to submission for 3 of those hours. I kept pushing for one more drill. Pushing past my burning body, my breath that was hard to catch, past the sweat pouring down.

I showered and rested until the next Jiu Jitsu class. Jiu Jitsu was great. I rolled as smart as I could. I tried many new things and felt proud of myself after. Despite my takedown being called out for being too complicated. I decided I wasn't defeated. I learned another takedown.

Paired with Cody, things ran smoothly. I understood longer sequences than I ever had. I was happy.

Rolls ran well too. It was all coming together.

We still had a few minutes after class and before the gym closed, to free roll. I asked for more.

Before we began, it snuck up on me.

Something in my body broke. I felt it. Suddenly I dropped to the floor, I couldn't stand up. Caught myself kneeling. The lights began to fade in and out. I felt so weird. Rolls of tension and pressure rode my body like a pissed off bull.

I couldn't get up. I closed my eyes and tried to calm myself, but the waves kept coming.

"Are you ok?" I heard Chance ask. I wanted to be brave so I said, "I have a lot of medical issues."

Then the shakes began. Left arm, right arm, until I was chicken winged to my chest. I fell back. The shakes gained intensity. A fellow Jiu Jitsu friend, voicing he was a doctor, offered water. I tried to nod, but as I did, my whole body began to shake. He went into doctor mode.

His hands grasped my ankles, and shook my legs as my upper body convulsed.

Out of the corner of my eye I saw Allen coming over. I closed my eyes in embarrassment. Trying to stop the shakes. My whole body convulsed.

"What is happening?!!" my heart cried.

"Put your hands on the floor," Allen's knowing voice said.

"Calm down, listen to him, it's the only way out." my mind said.

"Put your arms back and raise up. You're shaking because your arms don't know what to do."

"I can't!" I cried.

"Yes you can," he said firmly.

Slowly, like I was moving through quicksand, I lowered my hands to the mat. I ached, burned, hurt to my bones.

"Hold behind your knees."

This wasn't like my normal seizures. This was bad.

I struggled to stay conscious. The pressure waves continued.

The rest is blurry.

I know I made it out of the ring and onto the couch.

I know my friend was by my side.

I know I made a joke about cooties when offered a sports drink.

I know when the lights went out and it was just me and Allen, I began to break.

"What is this?!" my quivering voice asked.

"Rhabdomyolysis, it's when you push your body past what it can physically do. It shuts down. No more 8-hour training days. 2 hours, that's it."

I argued. "But I still have tomorrow and Friday to train!"

"Your body can't handle it Leslie."

I hung my head.

"How long is this going to last?"

"Depends on the person. Tonight, is going to suck for you. Your body will heal, but it will change after this."

"I have to get up and get to my car," I said.

"Yeah, you do," Allen said with a tone that said he was waiting for me to find that answer.

"It's so far." I just wanted to be cocooned in my blankets in my bed. Too many hard surfaces to get there. Hard car seat, hard concrete to walk on. Everything hurt so bad.

I took a breath, and stood. Somehow, I got my bags, and we made it outside where I grabbed a post, hung my head, and my tears fell.

I couldn't even cry without it hurting. They came in spurts of energy my body didn't want to lose. It didn't want to do anything.

"Welcome to being an athlete. We've all been through this. More than once."

"It's going to happen again?!"

"Only if you push yourself this far again. You're going to be ok. I'm being nonchalant because I've seen this happen many times. Go home, stay in the bath till the water becomes cool. Your body needs hydration. It won't hold anything in. Suck on ice overnight. You won't sleep, but you'll get through it."

I stepped, one burning leg after the other, as he walked me midway to my car. The handle was hard. My grip was weak. I smoked a little weed before going home, it helped take the edge off the pain. Somehow, I made it home. Pulling myself up the stairs by the railing. I did exactly as he said.

A bath had never hurt before. My body began to swell as it absorbed the water through its pores. My stretched skin hurt. Everything hurt. I sipped on juice, but my stomach rumbled. I wanted to puke.

I didn't sleep. I waited out the night in what felt like a pressurized ship in a bottle. Waves of weird sensations rode my body inside and out. Tingles, convulsions, the effects went on through the night.

I let my tears seep as crying hurt too much. I prayed, hard.

"God I need You so badly right now," my heart cried.

"I'm always here dear Daughter," God spoke kindly. *"This too shall pass,"* my mind reminded me.

My mind found its way to Jesus' torture. How bad that must have hurt. I felt rotten for causing it.

Before my heart could break over the newfound compassion I had for Jesus' pain, God swooped in with healing words.

"Leslie, I wanted that pain. That pain gave me you. It was worth it."

I had no words.

I have love.

I have Him.

He has me.

This is how God writes happy endings. By bridging the gap between the broken pieces.

Worth it.

6.27

Carry On

Dear Diary,

"How are you feeling?" Allen asked the next day after I stubbornly went to class.

"About 20%. My body still burns."

Allen suggested emailing the tournament and telling them about my condition as it was fairly risky to compete.

I'll test myself tomorrow in rolls. Past the drop-out deadline, but it gives me more time to heal.

"I do have good news," I said.

"I made my first business cards today for the tournament. It's getting real."

He smiled.

"Don't lose the momentum."

6.28

D-Day

Dear Diary,

I pulled out, I had to.

My body beat me before I could tap. I had nothing, I got nothing. My body was done. I tapped more times today than I ever have.

I seized again, with Shelby. My body is still broken.

As it started, my hand had been on Shelby's leg for a knee pass through guard. I clinched my hand on his leg to stabilize. He moved it to the floor. My feelings were hurt, but he was right. I needed to do it on my own.

After the seizure was over, Shelby and Carl had a long talk with me.

"You need to set goals, not expectations for yourself. Expectations are goals with deadlines. Goals come in their own time. Stop doing this to yourself Leslie," Shelby said.

He was right.

Sweet Carl was too. "Sometimes being brave means simply making the right decision. Nothing big or extravagant, just knowing what you need to do, and doing it, is brave. Especially when it's not what you want to do. Trust yourself and your body, it will tell you what you need to do. Then you will eventually be where you want to be."

It took them 2 hours, but eventually I listened to them and my body, and agreed to pull out of the tournament.

With trembling fingers, I sent the email before I left the gym. Knowing if I waited. I wouldn't do it.

"I feel like a failure. All this training, all this pain, for nothing now. I am weak," my heart cried.

"You did the right thing," Carl and Shelby said.

"You are doing the right thing," my mind said.

I am still going to go watch. It will be worth it.

6.29

The Right Fight

Dear Diary,

Spoiler Alert

Today's entry will be a bit rough as I don't want to change much from the raw realness. Throughout the day I lived and wrote as I saw. As you will see. I wanted to capture everything.

Once Upon a Good Fight...

I'm 30 years old, sitting in the parking lot of the first Jiu Jitsu tournament, I get to see. My name is Leslie Dawn.

I'm nervous, a bit disappointed I am too hurt to fight, but happy. It's a new door, and it fits me.

Hands trembling with excitement, I opened my car door. The black asphalt looked more like a red carpet to my fairytale eye. I smiled. I stood up in the sunlight.

"I'm so happy!" my heart exclaimed.

"Wow" I breathed.

"This is where you are meant to be," my mind saw from its 3rd eye.

I walked, grinning, down the sloping red carpet to the door of the event center. My heart beat and my hands trembled with excitement. As my feet stepped up onto the sidewalk, I spotted my best friend Danyce.

"Hey girl!" hugs were given to her, her husband, and all 4 of her cute kids.

"Are you excited?" she asked.

"Yes! Still kinda wish I was fighting but that will come in time," I replied.

"How do you feel?"

"Like I'm recovering from the flu. My body is still weak and I get weird muscle spasms and cramps often. Can't sleep either, but I'll get better. I'm at about 50% me."

"Yeah you will. Maybe it's better for you to just sit and write that way next time when you fight, you'll know what to look for your story. This time, you can help me sell our shirts."

Her and her husband had started a Jiu Jitsu shirt business with designs they had created. Looked like Jiu Jitsu meets graffiti to me. I made a mental note to buy one.

We chatted as we waited. Soon the doors were unlocked, and the best day of my life thus far, began.

Danyce ran ahead to talk set up with the coordinators, while we hung out in the lobby. Within a few minutes she literally ran back, eyes wide and bright.

"Dude, you're still on the bracket!" My heart dropped. Or took flight. I couldn't tell.

"Wait what? What is a 'bracket'?"

"The fight line up list. Your name is still on it! You're fighting today!"

"Oh shit!" my heart said.

"Oh shit!" I said.

"Oh yes!" my mind knew.

I could only stare, open mouthed, as my mind ran down a hallway of questions.

Could I fight, in my weakened condition?

Would I fight?

Should I fight?

Is it dangerous?

Is it fair to fight at not my best self?

Is this a test to see if I will fight, or know when to bow out?

What's the worst that could happen?

What's the best that could happen?

"What are you going to do?" Danyce asked.

"I don't know," my voice quivered.

"Can your body handle it?"

"I don't know," I repeated.

"The adrenaline will help, I promise. It will make you stronger."

"Can I hurt myself worse?"

"No," she said. "You'll just need a little longer to recover. But after this, a few more days resting will be worth it."

"Come on Leslie I know you can do it," her husband Efrain said. He was a great coach. I'd seen the way he coached their blooming daughter Kaylee. Gentle, firm, and always saw the best.

"You have enough training. Just do what you know. The best part of being a white belt is no one knows what you know. It's a place to have fun and try things out. No one will expect, or be disappointed in you. It's a safe place," he said.

"You got this girl," Danyce grinned. "You know you want to," she playfully nudged me with her elbow. "You know you didn't drive 3 hours here just to sit on the sidelines. Not now, not with your name on the bracket. That's your sign."

She was right, but I was still afraid.

"I need to talk to God," I said.

I wandered off, eyes on a world within my mind. Tears blurred the sun as I walked onto the sidewalk outside.

I told God how afraid I was, of fighting at all, but especially as weak as I was. I told Him I wasn't sure where He wanted me to go. Be strong or bow out. The rest of the prayer is too personal to type. As I stood in silence waiting for His answer, my heart began to speak.

"How many different ways are you going to tell yourself you can't? Or won't? Or shouldn't? You can't say you can't because you haven't tried yet. You've just stopped yourself before you've taken the first step. You can't say you won't because choice can change that. You can't say you shouldn't because you know you should. If you don't, you'll just be making the same choice not to fight, like you did all those years. That was a mistake, right? Don't make it again. Here no one can hurt you like he did. Here, both sides win. Here yall all walk away as Jiu Jitsu family. Your name is on the bracket, Leslie, how much more of a sign do you think you need?"

"What are you going to do, Leslie?" my mind asked.

"Say, yes," I said.

I smiled. Danyce grinned as I walked back in.

"You're going to do it aren't you?!"

"Yes," I said, voice quivering less with nerves and more with excitement now.

"I knew you would. I knew you had it in you. You're stronger than you think you are."

"That's what everyone says," I said.

"Yay! Leslie's going to fight her first fight!" Efrain cheered and fist bumped me.

"Yes I am," I declared.

...

Putting my business cards on their check-in table was one of the best feelings I'd ever felt. A step of faith towards my dream I could see and touch. Amazing.

I weighed in at 153. Was told the rundown, the rules, and to have fun.

I studied the rules for a few minutes, fearing being disqualified more than losing.

We set up their shirt stand, and then I explored.

...

What the movies can't show, is the feeling in the air. I'd never felt a buzz of excitement like this. Excitement, strength, pride, and a tight sense of family. Jiu Jitsu family. Felt like home to me.

The mat looks bigger than in the movies. But then again that could be my own mind. Everything looks different in person. It's blue, I'd imagined black.

The lights are dim. Giant fluorescent lights 3 stories above. Not the glaring spotlight of the movies. Still feels like they are shining on me. Is that prideful?

The people look normal. Moms saying "Don't run!" Dads getting gear and gi's ready. Tiny fighters as young as what looked like 6, play fighting on the mat. Tweens and teens in their friendship circles. A few 20-somethings in a world within their earbuds, stretching and thinking. I wonder if they were giving themselves pep talks. Very few adults. I supposed because adulthood and life meant arriving later when our matches actually began. Referees in black clothing, looking like with one glance they could kick my ass. They were all just, people. Improving their Jiu Jitsu skills on their own. Coming together to help each other up the podium. Families, friends, and now I am one of them. One of us.

Had you told me in high school as I watched martial arts movies over and over, that I would one day be one of them, I would have laughed. But here I am. Outside my training ground, in an unknown world that feels like home. Feels like I'm reliving my mirror moment at Ernie Reyes. That moment when I looked up, and saw it was me.

....

These little girls are as beautiful as they are fierce. Their moves have an overlying intensity to them. Like a hummingbird's wings. Beating so fast you can't see them move.

Their daddies watch them compete. Some smiling in pride, others pursing their lips as they study and coach.

"Underhook!" "Slide your knee up!" "You've got this sweetie!"

"I'm so proud of you!"

"I wish I had that," my heart ached a little.

"You do, with Me," God said.

"Stay focused on what you have," my mind guided.

One blonde girl tapped, then she cried. With tears streaming down her little 8-year-old face, she fought her next round.

"That's beautiful, that's strength. I want to be like her," my heart beamed.

"You are," God said.

"It's already within you," my mind knows.

...

Knowing I'd be even weaker without food, I decided to splurge on a treat: chili nachos, a pickle, and popcorn.

My taste buds were happy, my body was rejuvenated, and I was having the time of my life.

...

Today is a dream. I just read my children's book, to my best friend's daughter. She sat on my knee, and I read her my story. This story, this book, written as a fairytale for little girls.

"I'm so happy I could cry!" my heart shouted.

God smiled.

"You've earned this," my mind said.

...

The hours are flying by and the adult women are streaming in. Badass women. Women with fire in their eyes, muscles for days, and a vibrating strength I wish I had.

As my eyes took them in, God began to speak.

"You are one of them too, Leslie. You have that strength. Look how far you've come, look at what you have overcome."

I stood a little taller, my shoulders went from slumped to strong, and I smiled.

"That's My Girl."

...

Round and round the mat I walk, where I will stop, even I don't know. I'm praying near constantly. Battling my fears, battling my mind, pride, all of it.

I keep asking God to take away any pride I have. It's not me doing this. It wasn't me that caused the computer to keep my name. It wasn't me that brought my best friend to this event. Had she not been here, I likely would have chickened out. God knew I needed her. He is giving me everything I need.

I just want it to be Him they see. I want to live a story only He could author.

...

Adult call to rules. It's getting real.

Nerves are setting in. My heart is racing, my hands are cold. I am afraid.

"Is that what this is?" my heart questioned.

"It's your choice," God said.

"Fear, by any other name, would feel the same," my mind wisened.

I am excited.

I sat with a small group of women to hear the rules. 2 teens, and a woman who looked to be about my age. They smiled the most.

Kim, the woman my age, Kiera, a 16-year-old brown haired girl, and Kayla, her 14-year-old sister, a freckle faced blonde.

"Is this your first tournament?" asked Kim.

"Yes, is it that obvious?" I asked.

She laughed. "Only to someone who knows what to look for."

"They are so much fun!" Kayla said.

"We've done a lot of them," her sister Kiera said.

"How do you fight the nerves?" I asked.

Kim spoke up. "You realize this isn't a fight against someone, but a test for yourself. At the end of the day we are all family and friends. At the end of the match, you'll have learned more about yourself. That's where the win is." Kim's eyes held mine for a moment. Piercing the truth of her words into me with her knowing stare.

"Just have fun and enjoy the ride." she said. I smiled.

...

Likely my last chance to give myself a pep talk, I went to the far side of the giant room, behind the giant curtain. I knelt. I prayed. I am not writing the dialogue of my prayer as they were intimate words between me and God.

After my words with God were spoken, I looked up the words to my favorite pep talk of all time. The one Herb Brooks gave to his 1980 U.S. Men's Olympic hockey team before they played and beat the Soviets.

They, like me, were up against insurmountable odds. Who am I to think I can beat PTSD? Who were they to think they could beat the Soviets? Gold medalists for 5 out of the last 6 Olympics. PTSD a battle fought for life. We both had dragons to fight.

Belief, changed everything. It turned a possibility, into a probability, into a miracle.

I watched, on my glowing little phone screen, in the darkened room.

My eyes blurred with tears, my skin got Godbumps, and my heart spoke.

"I want that. I want to be brave. I want to be strong."

"Go out there, and be the best Leslie," God said.

"Go out there be brave, be strong. This is your time, your moment. What are you going to do?" my mind asked.

"I am going to take it," I said.

"Are you good?" I heard Efrain's voice. Looked up, he was walking over. "You're not talking yourself out of it are you?"

I smiled.

"No, I was giving myself a pep talk."

He smiled.

"You got this girl. You can do it. Believe in yourself. I do, Danyce does. You're about to live the best moment of your life, choosing to fight. Choosing to fight back for fun. You've already won by being here, unlike the rest of the women, sitting at home. What's there to lose?"

I smiled.

"Thanks coach."

He smiled.

"Let's go!"

"This is my moment," my heart whispered.

"This is your time," my mind shouted.

"This is mine," I said.

…

Kayla, the freckle faced blonde who looks more like she should be pedaling a bicycle with a basket of flowers, rather than fighting, excitedly ran up to me as I rounded the curtain.

"I'm your match!"

My jaw dropped. I didn't want to fight someone so sweet.

"Um, wow."

"I volunteered."

She wanted this. She wanted me. It was all in good fun for her. It was then I knew my mind needed to change. It wasn't a fight. It was fun. It was family.

I smiled. I grinned. She grinned back.

…

Before I knew it, our names were being called. The room began to fade. I saw only the blue mat, my road to a happy ending.

It wasn't until later, when I watched the videos, I heard the encouraging words of Danyce, Efrain, Kim, Kiera, and the girls' sweet mother Michelle.

My heart roared. A grin covered my face. As my bare feet stepped onto the mat, a flood rushed me. I don't know what the rush was, but it was real, and it was sweet.

Kayla and I stood, the ref between us. Just like in the movies, but this was better. I could feel it. It was me in the ring. Life is better in person.

"Fight!"

The next minute flew by in a whirlwind of adrenaline, fun, fantastic-ness. My mind quieted, and I did what I knew. My body, my training, my drills, took control. I didn't have to make decisions, I just did.

My only goal in mind was to get the takedown, my greatest fear. I did.

She got me in a tight triangle. I tapped.

...

She had won the match. I had won more of me.

...

I wanted more. After the first round, after the first rush, I wanted to do it again.

As I stepped off the mat, I knew I had changed. 60 seconds to change Leslie.

Excited voices met me like a verbal hug.

"How was it?! How do you feel? Wasn't it awesome?!" Danyce, Kim, and Efrain surrounded me, grins and eyes glowing like they knew something I didn't.

"THAT WAS SO MUCH FUN!" I nearly shouted. "I want to do it again!"

I heard cheers.

"You get to in your second round! Girl it ain't over yet!"

...

Dalton, the younger brother of the girls, wanted to be in my book. So here is his shout out. Dalton, here you are. I love you like another little brother of mine. I can't wait to choke you with my hair again.

....

Round 2, Kayla got me in a rear naked. A tinge of disappointment I had lost again, was quickly washed away by pride. Pride I was fighting. I was fighting, for fun.

My mind flashed to an image of me standing in the middle of a tornado. A tornado I had created with the whiplash of turning around so fast, to fight my dragon. All this time I had been running backwards, facing and fighting the dragon of my past, while believing I was moving forwards. I was, in a way, but I couldn't see my beautiful future, as I had turned my back on it. The tornado shredded, the eye closed, and the flashes of memories and tears of my past fell like ash to the green grass my bare feet now stood on. The sun beamed, spotlighting me. I smiled, and turned around. Ahead I saw a vanishing horizon, bursting with all the colors of sunrises, rainbows, and sunsets. Beneath the mosaic sky, the earth glowed with green grass, as yellow daisies danced over top. Beginning at my feet, the yellow petaled road, spread in every direction. Ahead of me, a thin glimmering line, split the ground from the sky. The finish line. In my mind, I began to run. Run towards that sparkly line. Over the ground I flew, chest bursting with as many new happy feelings as there were colors in the magnificent sky. It felt like I began to fly. I no longer cared what was behind me. What I saw in front of me, was better than anything I remembered. My view had changed. My life, had changed. The definition of fighting had taken new meaning: I wasn't fighting against my dragon; I was fighting for me.

I know this fight for myself will never end. I know the PTSD will creep up on me, in the most inopportune moments. I know it will attack me. I also know, I will fight it, every time. I can't erase my past. I can, and will, never stop fighting, and smiling.

...

I'll never forget, standing on the podium for the first time. I felt higher than I ever had. Above Cloud 9. I bowed, and a silver medal was hung around my neck. I stood up, strong. Tears finally flowing.

I didn't care who was watching. Once they read my story, they would know the tears were worth it.

"This is the best moment of my life!" I blubbered. Through the blur of tears, I saw a woman, smiling and watching me. I hoped I was inspiring her.

Cameras flashed; my new Jiu Jitsu family stood round. I smiled bigger than I ever knew I could.

I had done it.

From bruised to badass.

From fear to fun.

From "I can't" to "I did."

From fairytales to dreams.

I made my reality.

Do you believe in miracles?

I do.

THE HAPPY NEVER ENDINGS

THANK YOU LETTERS

Dear Prince Charming,

Thank you. Thank you, for everything you did. Thank you for believing bloodying and bruising me was the right thing to do. Notice I didn't say "beat," my dear Beast. You did not and cannot beat me.

If I had it to do all over again, I'd trap your arms, step in a big circle, elbow you in your face, slide step back, and front kick you as hard as I could in your dick. I'd then knee check, and re-stand my ground and stance. After that, I'd probably smile, in pride. All this I would do the very first time.

Then I'd leave you, hurt on the floor, as you so often did me. Don't worry, you'd heal and eventually get over it, like I learned how to do. I'd pack my bags, and leave your ass. The first time.

Don't try me. I now have a very unique set of skills. I will not make the first move, as there is no first attack in self-defense. But if you do, honey, just don't, just don't.

Just so you know I'm not mad at you. Never was. Coulda woulda shoulda been, but I'm not.

I don't love you anymore either. Fond of, yeah I guess, but I would not take a bullet for you, I wouldn't give you a second chance, and I finally know not to trust anything you say or do. You were a dragon, a living nightmare, you were the hardest and worst part of my life.

I took the shit you gave me, and put it in a compost pile where it fed my seeds of hope and belief. Buds that burst through the dark earth. Stems that grew in the sun's all-seeing rays. Flowers that burst into bloom. Now I have a rainbow garden of goodness with the shit you gave me. I couldn't have done it without you.

Now I love me too.

Thank you.

L

Dear Kat Bradshaw,

I'll never forget meeting you at Ernie Reyes way back when I was in high school. I'll never forget seeing your beautiful photography work. I'll never forget telling you then, someday, in the future, I wanted you to take my wedding pictures. I'll never forget, 10 years later, you finally did.

I finally got to run in a field, in a white dress. I finally got to feel like a Princess. The ethereal glow of your work, which I had fallen in love with so long ago, helped hide the pain, I felt that day. You took some photos I still cherish, despite the unhappy ending.

I'll never forget, though it hasn't happened yet, our happy ending. As the years have passed your work has deepened its glow, and now we are at the point you get to shoot my happy beginning. In the coming weeks you are going to shoot my book cover, as well as other storytelling shots me and my training partner Autumn are coming up with. This time my smile won't have to hide my pain. This time I truly am happy. The best part of my life is about to begin.

You are one of the few people there from my martial arts beginning to my new me beginning. I love our story. I love your work. I love your kindness and willingness to help me. Thank you so much Kat. I know I'll love the new photos coming soon.

I can't wait to see what happens next.

L

Dear Prydacted, Carl, Autumn, Shelby, Mitchell, Lucas, Chance, Andrew (both of them), Tyler, Patrick, Chad, Cody, and everyone else from Allen's gym,

Thank yall for helping me on this barefooted road. I know I have been difficult, and arguably shed too many tears in full view of yall. Thanks for not giving up on me. Thanks for the advice, talks, and vent sessions. I hope this book helps yall see it was all worth it in the end.

Some of yall's stories have yet to be told, but I promise one day they will be. It is much earned and much deserved.

Thank yall so much for helping me get to my happy life. The best is yet to come.

L

Dear Allen,

Thank you. Thank you for being my hero. Thank you for the countless hours of therapeutic talks. Thank you for leading me on this barefooted road I didn't know where to go.

I could have done it without you, but I know I wouldn't have. I would have tried. Would have dove deep inside my head and heart to try and find the puzzle pieces of truth you gave me. I probably would have gotten dizzy and frustrated, and given up. Given in to the victim mentality. I would have found a husband to join my lifelong pity party, and stayed there. Content to live a life with him looking down on me in love and sympathy. At least it would have been something. It would have been easy. I like this story better.

The last year and a half has been the hardest, scariest, and most rewarding time of my life. I'm sure I drove you crazy at times. Thank you for not giving up on me. Kind of ironic that you as the strongest man I know, were dealt the craziest woman I know. Thank you for helping me calm my storm.

Had you told me, when I first saw you at 16, all those dreams and feelings of wanting to be you, would come true, I probably would have nervously giggled in your face. Nervousness hiding the hope it was true. I now feel the bravery, confidence, power, strength, and zeal coming from within, thanks to you.

I feel like I'm there. I feel like a heroine.

Now, like I've watched you do for so long, I want to inspire and bring out the best in people through martial arts. I want to change the whole world, beginning with the martial arts world.

Words cannot accurately describe how flattered, grateful, honored, humbled, and gifted I feel by all you have done for me.

It's not every day people get to meet, greet, and get to know their hero. But I did. It's not in every lifetime people get rescued by their hero, but I did.

God saved me. Allen, you'll always be my hero.

L

TIME CAPSULES

Dear Ladies,

I wish I could tell you love doesn't hurt, but it does. It hurts because when you love, you give a part of yourself up. To a person, a dream, an idea, not knowing if it will come back to fruition. I can tell you, when it does come home, it comes back bigger and better than what you gave up. That's the full circle of a heart. It's worth it all.

What they don't tell you, is you can change the pain. A pain by any other name still feels the same. The difference in cost and loss is whether or not we decide the ending or goal we can't see, is worth it, or not. In cost, we are simply giving what is needed, to get what we dream of. In loss, we see only what we are missing, not what could be coming. The choice, the view, is up to us. We can change the pain from lost, to cost.

I can tell you, all the pain I survived, all the tears I cried, all the flashbacks I saw behind my eyes, the last year and a half of intense internal fight, were all worth it, to get here. You can be here too. You just have to fight, to set your sights on the vanishing horizon, and go. One barefooted step at a time. Don't give up, my dear ladies.

Those men took enough life from our past. We can't let them take our happiness from our future. We can't let them beat us within our heads and hearts. We need to become strong, we need to fight, we need to live, laugh, and love, us. We can do this together.

In my wildest dreams, I imagine this book bringing the world of women together, as fighters, something never before seen in history. I dream an American Dream of red hearts, white wings, and blue tears. We women fighting for ourselves on the mats of martial arts. Helping, holding, and healing ourselves, together. We need to find each other, find our girl squad, our bff, a life coach, someone we can go-to to help us through this journey.

I know we can do it, because I did it. Me, a bedwetting, former backrow Baptist, battered but not beaten, pity party pro hostess did it. What did I do? I chose to fight, knowing the dragon will always be there. I chose to love myself, all the pieces I no longer call broken because I know I am not broken. I am Leslie. I chose to never give up, to never stop believing, living and loving.

Say the three-letter word that changes life, ladies. Say "Yes!" Sign up for martial arts, get a life coach, get a girl squad, and fight for yourself.

This is my life, I'll cry, fight, smile if I want to. Yall can too. I believe in each and every one of you. Love yall.

L

Dear Leslie,

You did it.

L

MY CLEAN LITTLE VICTORIES

Summer 2017
A Helping Hand
Dear Diary,
I cried today, happy tears, over my bedwetting.

I arrived at a jobsite of an elderly lady. During the night she had gotten up to get some water, fallen, and was unable to get back up. She lay on the kitchen floor all night, and wet herself. Her son found her the next morning. As the job instructions were given, she sat in a kitchen chair, waiting for her son to take her to the hospital. I looked in her eyes, and recognized what she was feeling: shame.

I knelt in front of her, took her hand, looked into her eyes, and with tears in my own, asked, "Ma'am, would you like me to wash you off before you go to the hospital?" Relief flooded her face. I stood, tears freely falling down my face. Into her ear I whispered, "I know how you feel. I've been wetting the bed most of my life." Her eyes filled, and her lips smiled. We cried together for a moment as I held her. United together in our not so secret shame.

My coworker and I got her back to her bedroom, where I washed her clean. Far beyond my call of work duty, and arguably a fireable offense. I didn't care about my job, I cared about her. She calmed and warmed as we put clean clothes on her.

Before walking her back to the kitchen, she pulled me to her, and with happy tears in her eyes, said, "Thank you." I knew what she meant, and what I had just done. We held each other one more moment, and cried happy tears together.

Several hours later, on my way home, I cried again, talking to my mom on the phone.

"My bedwetting finally helped someone mom! It was such an incredible day! In a way it feels like all my years of pain were worth it for the help and relief it gave her! It finally feels like my bedwetting meant something. I finally got something out of it. I got to help."

The funny thing about happy endings, is we never know when they are going to happen.

Spring 2020
A Different Hand
Dear Diary,

I used to think it was God, who stopped my bedwetting. I used to think it was the "sign" I'd been waiting for. I'm older, smarter, and wiser now. I now believe it was Satan.

The best lie Satan has been able to convince us of, is that he and God are in a duo-deitied war. That they are equals. People forget, God made Satan too. He is just a runaway angel. He has no creationistic power. There is no such thing as black magic. All he can do, is blind us. Blind us with darkness, lies, cancer cells that create walls to block bodily functions, and squirrels to keep us distracted for days.

I believe, it was God who let my piss flow, and Satan who cured me by building a wall to stop it. God knew what both of them were doing, to what end even I don't know yet.

I think Satan somehow knew what my Beast was going to do to me, and knew the fastest way to get me there, was to get me to fall. Fall out of my senses and my head, via the emotional freedom I felt with my cure. I was blind from the beginning. Because I trusted my human feelings, more than my eternal mind.

If I listen closely, I believe I can hear the echoes of what God was saying to me all those years I cussed Him out for causing my bedwetting.

"Thank you for talking to Me, My Daughter. I know and feel your pain. Trust Me, I have a master plan. The pain will pay off in the end."

Though I do not know what the ending is, I do know I have found some happy, in my secret shame story. As of now, my bedwetting comes and goes. Though it doesn't hurt me like it used to. I have accepted it as part of me. As part of the whole me. I now know I am not broken because part of me doesn't work as I think it should. God still loves me, diapers and all.

Summer 2020
The Best Medicine
Dear Diary,

Allen, Shelby, and myself were sitting in the ring talking after class one day. Therapy in full session, it was Shelby who delivered another happy ending.

Disclaimer: due to me not wanting to mess with copyright permissions, I'm not going to tell the actual nerd movie name he used. Perhaps I will in the future, but right now, I ain't got time fo dat paperwork.

Shelby, in his best valley girl voice, tossed his long shiny hair over his shoulder, cocked his hand on his hip and said, "Girl you just need to get yourself some **** **** boxers to cover up that diaper in style."

I laughed. From his perfect imitation, to the crazy awesome idea he had just given me, I laughed, about my bedwetting, for the first time in my life.

It felt like freedom.

Near happy tears, I readily agreed to his idea. After class to the store I went, but not before Allen spoke a few words.

In what looked and felt like the closest persona to a big brother I had seen from him, he clenched his fist. His voice carried care, mild aggravation at the countless hours he himself had spent trying to help me get to the point Shelby had just brought me to, and what sounded like an adulting life challenge, he said, "If you come back from this, I'm going to punch you."

It wasn't until later I realized what he meant. He knows I slip and slide back into old habits and mentalities, all too easily. I start running in a new direction before I get my balance and footing. He was reminding me I needed to stay strong.

Would he punch me if I were to fall back? Yeah, probably. But with the right amount of force to punch me back on track.

I bought the boxers. Far too small as I was confused on men's sizing. I muffin topped them anyway.

I smiled wearing a diaper that night. Then I cried happy tears.

DANCING WITH LIGHTNING

July 7, 2020
Dear Diary,
 I danced with lightning this morning.
 Into my wedding dress I stepped. For the first time since our unhappy ending. I was planning on waiting, waiting until my book cover photo shoot. I decided I needed a moment alone, to accept the life I had lived.
 My heart was pounding, my tears ready to fall, in my mind I saw flashbacks, of it all. I was so scared.
 Corset tied tight, it barely fit around my now small waist. I turned and looked in the mirror, face to my face.
 I smiled. I looked beautiful. I felt, beautiful. Not what I was expecting.
 I was expecting pain from a life unlived. Memories unmade. Dreams, forever trapped in never-ever day.
 I got, happy. I got Godbumps. I got a second chance.
 I danced. I danced to songs about butterflies and kisses, Cinderella and love. Twirling in my bedroom alone, glitter falling like lightning from my life, I danced.
 I realized I didn't need a man to make my memories. I could twirl by myself, no man's toes needed stepped on. I could balance alone.
 I felt God smiling at me. I imagined Jesus dancing with me.
 I briefly imagined dancing with my dad, until that image caused me pain, so I swept it away. I nearly got lost in that loss, until I decided that's not where I needed to stay. I had better things in front of my face. I could say yes, to a better happy ending, with myself.
 I cried, I cried happy tears. I cried for the freedom of feeling happy in my wedding dress. Happier than my pretend wedding day. This time, there was no reason to hide. No plastic smile. No hoping for a better life. I could look in the mirror, and smile.
 I don't know for how long I twirled. I do know, I finally felt like the little 8-year-old Leslie girl. Twirling and dreaming.

Prince Charming's face once before unseen, now, not needed. I don't need a man to make me a Queen.

I am a Queen, by simply being ruler of me. By taking ownership of my decisions, my life, my mind.

It's my life, I'll fly and shine if I want to.

LOVE'S NEVER ENDING

The Beautiful Picture
Dear Diary,

When I look at the shape of a broken heart, I see the meaning of life.

Starting at the bottom pointy part of the heart, I see a story. I see a Loveline. I see God, at our beginning; life as soon as our lives are created. As we live our timeline, we go up the straight side of the heart. As ourselves and our minds grow, we begin to see. Our sight, and our choices, create the curve, as we begin to decide for ourselves. Life goes in the direction we decide.

If we decide, to turn around, and begin the journey back to where we came from, the footsteps begin. That's the zigzag heartbroken line: footsteps, one after another, heading home. The way home, is aCross.

I believe home is in Love, in God. In the realm where all the things we feel, we can finally see. I believe, after we die, we cross that heartbroken line, to the other side. We will finally see the full circle of the heart. I can only imagine what that mirror image looks like. What a wonderful world that must be.

Choose Heaven
Dear Diary,

I believe, when we die, we still get to decide. The Bible never says we run out of time, to change our minds.

I believe one of the first things we will see, is God looking at us, smiling. You see, when God as Love, looks at us, I believe He will see Himself: the image of Himself He made us to be. When God as the Judge, God still as Love, looks at us, I believe no set of scales will be seen. Judges look at both sides, calculating evidence to determine guilty, or innocent. Our Judge God, our

Love God, I believe, won't, because He can't. Love doesn't do that. Love accepts, Love sees the best, Love pulls in, Love wants us with Him.

Hate, pushes away. If our God were a God of hate, He would send us to hell. But He won't, because that's not what Love does.

I don't believe in hell, at least not the external and inescapable prison lake of fire we imagine it to be. I stayed up all night one night, looking at every single Bible verse using that word. I traced them back to the original language, found the original definitions, and none of them described hell how we imagine it today. Maybe someday I'll draw a diagram with all the definitions and things I found. But for now, it's up to you to choose to believe me, or not.

I believe, after the moment God looks and sees all of us, smiling and loving us, we become our own Judge through the still freedom of choice. We get to choose, if we believe Him, if we want to spend eternity with Him, and if we accept Him too.

I believe hell exists within us. It is created in that moment, within our hearts, if we say "No," to the Love that made us. Denying ourselves, the truth of who we really are. I believe hell is the burning and tearing feeling we feel, when within our hearts, by walking away from the Love that made us, we kill our core. I believe hell is the bottomless pit we feel in our hearts, when we run from love and home, not knowing where to go. We all know the feeling of being lost, knowing we are headed in a direction to a dead end. We can't escape the draw of love, and we can't outrun home. Hell is homelessness, hell is lovelessness. It is created when we judge ourselves unforgivable and unworthy.

Every time I have walked away from God in my own life, my heart burned. Life didn't feel like home anymore. I felt lost in this existence. Purposeless save for myself. I was doing what I wanted for me. It was lonely and temporary. Rarely during those times did I cry into Jesus' chest. I was too ashamed. I thought He was disappointed in me. Though I do know that's when He wanted me the most. He would have held me close. But I couldn't and wouldn't see His Love through my self-inflicted pain. Hell is in the bottomless pit of a shadow I made when I turned from the Light of His face.

I believe, in that moment, in the moment we too get to choose to love God too, everyone will choose God. Who in their right mind wouldn't? Sure, there might be a few people who turn away blind. But I doubt it will take much time, for them to wisen and wake up and come back home.

I believe this is what love will do. I believe the best happy ending for all of eternity, is all of us together, as one big happy family. Like we were in the very beginning. It's the only part of history we haven't repeated. The full circle, of the heart.

Love hurts = Jesus wept

SATAN'S HAPPY ENDING

Prodigal Angel
Dear Diary,
The best Happily Ever After I can think of, isn't about me. It isn't about this story. It's about Satan. The lost little angel.

They say history repeats itself, but we have yet to repeat the beginning. Universal Peace. When we were all one big happy family.

In the wildest parts of my imagination, in the brightest of my daydreams, in the deepest depths of my heart, I have begun to believe.

I imagine, Satan going up to God, a lost sheepish look on his face. Tears streaming down his cheeks. Hands possibly folded in prayer, or wringing nervously. Though his nerves are of his own making. He already knows what God will say. I imagine him coming to God, after he had his coming to Jesus moment. God only knows what that moment will look like. This moment, the moment the prodigal angel comes home, I imagine, to sound like this:

"Dear God, will You forgive me too?"

I believe, before Satan can get his next words out, God will know his heart, and pull him in, as love does. Then, I imagine, God will say the one Word even Satan, can't deny.

"Mine."

Runaway angel
Come back home
There's a place for you at the table
Don't let it get cold
God's arms are open waiting
Love won't say no, to you
Runaway angel
You can't outrun home

My Happy Be

July 4th, 2020
The Be Me
Dear Diary,
I am happy. I am my reality.
My Happy Never-Ending, is me.

About the Author
I'm just a woman with a dream. A dream I'm making my reality, in Nashville, TN.